PUB WALKS
IN & AROUND
THE NEW FOREST

PETER CARNE

COUNTRYSIDE BOOKS
NEWBURY BERKSHIRE

First published in 1993 by
Ensign Publications

**This new updated edition
published in 1999 by**

COUNTRYSIDE BOOKS
3 Catherine Road
Newbury
Berkshire RG14 7NA

ISBN 1 85306 600 1

Maps by Jack Street
Photographs by Peter Carne
Cover photograph of Swan Green, Lyndhurst
supplied by Terry Heathcote

Produced through MRM Associates Ltd., Reading
Printed by Woolnough Bookbinding Ltd., Irthlingborough

Walk   •   CONTENTS   •   Page

• INTRODUCTION •

The New Forest is more popular with walkers than almost anywhere else in Britain, and there are many reasons for this. Its combination of picturesque ancient woodlands, extensive plantations of trees of many species grown for timber in fenced inclosures, and heathery moors where ponies wander at will has no equal elsewhere. Its wealth of wildlife offers never-failing interest to the naturalist, and the freedom it gives to roam almost anywhere is unrivalled.

With so much from which to choose it is helpful, especially to newcomers, to begin exploring the Forest by following well-tried routes such as those described in detail here. To add to the interest of each walk, background information is given about the locality concerned, together with a map reference of the starting-point, details of relevant Ordnance Survey maps and of how to get there either by car or by public transport. To help round off the pleasure of every individual outing, each walk starts and finishes at a licensed hostelry where the facilities available are summarised for your benefit. Information is also given about any pubs along the route where you may be tempted to call in for a pint and a pie.

The scenic variety of the New Forest itself goes with an even richer diversity in the country around its margins, so often neglected by Forest enthusiasts yet crying out for exploration. Many of the walks in this book provide an introduction to the delights of nearby downland, river valley and quiet coast.

All the walks are circular, most are a modest five or six miles long and so are well within the capacity of the average weekend walker. In some cases longer and shorter alternative routes are given, each being clearly defined on the accompanying sketch map. Robust footwear is strongly advised, especially following wet weather, and a walking stick can prove helpful to cope with occasional sticky patches and luxuriant vegetation. Remember to close all gates behind you, to leave no litter and to keep dogs under strict control at all times.

All routes have been re-walked and descriptions updated as necessary for this second edition. Information about maps, pubs, public transport and all other aspects has also been brought up to date. I hope you enjoy the walks as much as I have done while checking them out for your benefit — and my own.

PETER CARNE
Spring 1999

Quiet Countryside near Cadnam

WALK 1
Up to 3 hours
5 miles
Walk begins page 6

Background to the Walk

Cadnam, first recorded in 1272 as 'Cadenham' and apparently meaning 'homestead or enclosure of a man called Cada', has been slow to develop into a recognisable village despite its antiquity as a placename. It is not even a separate parish but, like Ower, Winsor, Newbridge and Bartley, lies within the parish of Copythorne, the name of which means 'cropped thorn' and is thought to relate to the ancient practice of pollarding, which involved trimming off side branches of certain trees as winter feed for forest deer.

Whereas Copythorne proper lies just outside the present New Forest, Cadnam is right on the edge of it, with extensive, scenic woodlands flanking the roads on its southern approaches. Such remnants of old time forest peace as may have lingered until recently have been swept into oblivion since the coming of the motorway, which looms high on an embankment directly behind the Sir John Barleycorn Inn to provide a striking confrontation between things ancient and modern.

In 1964 the Forest's boundary was extended to take in extensive commonlands between Cadnam and West Wellow along with the common rights still exercised by local owners of livestock. You skirt one of these, Cadnam Common, on the outward stage of this walk, which brings you to the edge of Bramshaw before swinging south to Brook.

Brook, with its two pubs, several thatched dwellings and situation near the source of the Cadnam River, whence its name, is a typically

Maps
Landranger 1:50,000
Sheets 184, 195 and 196
1:25,000
Outdoor Leisure 22 New Forest
Map Reference of Start/Finish
SU293136

How to get there
Cadnam lies just off the western end of M27 at the confluence of A31 from Romsey, Ferndown and Wimborne, A336 from Totton, A337 from Lyndhurst, and B3079 from Landford (joined by B3078 from Fordingbridge, which is joined in turn by B3080 from Downton). From Southampton head west along A3024, M271 and M27 to Cadnam, where you turn off and take the first exit. From Bournemouth follow the town centre bypass (Wessex Way), A338 and then eastbound A31 to the beginning of M27 at Cadnam and there filter left to take the third exit. From this take the first turning left (the service road for the Sir John Barleycorn) or continue to Cadnam roundabout and there turn left for the White Hart, a few yards along on the left, with car parking space at the front and the rear. Cadnam is served by Solent Blue Line/Wilts & Dorset buses on service X2 between Southampton, Ringwood and Bournemouth and services 31/31A between Southampton, Totton and Lyndhurst.

Pub facilities
White Hart, Cadnam

This hostelry traces its history back to AD1448. An earlier hostelry is supposed to have been a stopping-off place for Purkess (or Purkis), the charcoal-burner, when on his way to Winchester with the body of William Rufus. At a much later time it was a place of call for stagecoaches plying between London and Plymouth. It claims a ghost which makes its presence felt by the smell of heavily scented flowers in the oldest part of the building. Some original beams in the building's structure go with locally handmade Bartley bricks. Opening hours are 1100-1500 and from 1800-2300 on weekdays and 1200-1500 and 1800-2230 on Sundays. Home made traditional pub fare ranging from stews and casseroles in winter to salads in summer may be ordered between 1200-1400 and 1800-2130 until 2100 on Sundays. Brews include Boddington's, Flower's Original and Ringwood Best Bitter as well as Whitbread Best Bitter, Mild Ale, Murphy's Irish Stout, Guinness and draught cider. Barbecues and a skittle alley are other attractions. Children may use the large garden and may be admitted to the back room. Coach parties are catered for and well-behaved dogs on leads are not unwelcome. Walkers who use the pub may leave their cars in the large pub car park, but please ask first! Telephone: 01703 812277.

Sir John Barleycorn, Cadnam

Tracing its history as far back as the 12th century and even farther, this well known inn could well be the oldest pub in Hampshire and is certainly one of the most picturesque with its roof and doorway overhangs of

The Green Dragon, Brook

pleasant New Forest hamlet at the junction of two B roads and of a lane which winds south through woods to Rufus's Stone, where the Red King is said to have died. The story of how he went hunting one August day with some of his courtiers and became victim of an arrow possibly meant for a stag, or perhaps a boar, and loosed by one Sir Walter Tyrrell, is one of the best known in England's history, as is that of his subsequent journey to Winchester on the cart of a man named Purkess. Another theory has it, though, that he met his death near Beaulieu, so perhaps other oft-related details are the fruits of some embroidering of the facts of what actually happened 900 years ago.

You head back to Cadnam by way of Bignell Wood, an ancient tract of timber which shares its name with that of a house tucked away in the trees by the Cadnam River roughly halfway between Cadnam and Brook.

Walk 1

Distance: *Allow 3 hours for this five mile walk.*
Assuming a start at the Sir John Barleycorn Inn, follow Southampton Road east for a very few yards and then turn left to follow Old Romsey Road. Only a little way along this, turn left at a crossroads to follow

a lane which bridges the tree-shaded, gravel-bottomed Cadnam River. One of the smallest waterways in Hampshire to rate as a river, this receives Forest streams with names like King's Garn Gutter and Coalmeer Gutter before meandering north-east around Copythorne to Paultons Park, where it feeds a lake. Near Ower it ends its brief existence by merging its modest substance with that of the River Blackwater, a tributary of the Test.

Your lane passes under the M27 and crosses a cattlegrid flanked by a gate for walkers and riders. It then continues pleasantly as a tree-bordered, hedged byway alongside which ponies graze the verges as a reminder that you are still within the New Forest's official confines as decreed by an Act of Parliament passed in 1964. Disregard a lane that soon angles sharply right from a triangular intersection and carry on to where Springer's Farm House and its outbuildings lie to your right. Just beyond this you bear right at a fork of lanes with the buildings of Manor Farm on your left. The lane you now follow curves left before being joined from the right by a road signposted as leading to Storm's Farm only. Ignore this and carry on a few yards farther to where a house confronts you just to the right of where the public road becomes a private driveway leading on into Warren's Estate.

Just short of the house and its flanking open gateway fork right from the metalled road to follow a grass-centred track which is also a public footpath. Oak and holly-shaded banks enclose the unmetalled hollow lane you now follow north, downhill to where what soon becomes an earth track bridges a very minor stream. Beyond this the fringe of trees broadens into woodland, with oak, beech, holly and bracken spreading scenically to your right and mature oaks and hollies flanking tall larches to your left. Where Cadnam Common's open spaces come into view through the trees to your right the track forks. Here you continue left-ahead, then within a few yards turn left along a track which leads to a metal gate flanked by a stile on which is a yellow waymarking arrow. Here my companion and I found

thatch and its long, low, whitewashed frontage. Purkess the charcoal burner is claimed to have actually lived here (or perhaps in a previous inn on the same site?). Brews include Flower's Original, Boddington's, Castle Eden and, frequently, Wadworth 6X, as well as Whitbread Best Bitter, Murphy's Irish Stout and Heineken and Stella lagers. Strongbow cider is also on draught as well as two white wines. Six other selected white wines and six red wines are also available. Food ranges from steaks and crab and lobster to humble steak and kidney pie — always a favourite — and may be ordered between 1130 (1200 on Sundays) and 2130, opening hours being 1100-2300 (1200-2230 on Sundays). Telephone: 01703 812236.

Green Dragon Inn, Brook

This pub is where historian Dr Crawford from Southampton University once heard two local countrymen talking in a dialect not far removed from pure Saxon. Locals as well as visitors still congregate in the tile-floored New Forest Bar, the other bar, with its adjoining restaurant area, being carpeted. The 600-years-old thatched building has been a pub for about a century and opens from 1030-1500 and 1800-2300 on weekdays and from 1200-1500 and 1900-2230 on Sundays. Food, all home made, may be ordered between 1200-1415 and 1830-2100 on weekdays and from 1200-1430 and 1900-2100 on Sundays and ranges from ploughman's, sandwiches and jacket potatoes to mixed grills, chicken Kiev, fillet plaice and salmon shanties (salmon and broccoli in a creamy sauce). A full restaurant menu is also available. Telephone: 01703 813359.

The Bell Inn, Brook

A few yards farther along the road beyond The Green Dragon is this luxuriously appointed hostelry with a comfortable restaurant, a bar with an inglenook fireplace and beamed bedrooms in its oldest part. Opened in 1797 by ancestors of the present owners, who also own the adjacent Bramshaw Golf Club with its two 18-hole courses, as well as the course at Dunwood near Romsey. It specialises in good food, fine wines, and home comforts for residents. The bar is open from 1100-2300 on weekdays and from 1200-2130 on Sundays. Telephone: 01703 812214.

A roadside green just north of Cadnam

a seat to enjoy a picnic lunch.

Cross the stile to follow a green lane bordered by bracken and scrub. Where the green lane soon forks bear left and skirt left-handed of brackeny open ground to reach a fence preceding farmland. A few yards to the right of a metal gate here are two adjacent stiles. Cross the right-hand stile, where a notice says 'please keep to the public footpath', to enter a meadow in which you head diagonally right towards a gate flanked by a stile at its far right-hand corner. Blenman's Farm overlooks you from your right as you approach the stile, after crossing which you follow a fenced grass track which is soon joined from the right by the metalled lane serving Blenman's Farm. This lane leads ahead to a public road, grass-verged and tree-lined as you follow it left-handed. Grazing sheep and copper beeches in fresh leaf shared the road's green margin as we headed now south-west for half-a-mile to Bramshaw's outskirts.

Just short of Stock's Cross, where the road you now follow crosses the Brook-Landford road, turn left past Stock's Cross Lodge and through a gateless gateway to follow a metalled driveway which is also a public footpath. Rhododendron-flanked parkland embellished with cedar now spreads beside you, with Warren's House in view through trees to your left as you head south-east past a right-hand golf course. Disregard the first footpath signpost on your right and keep right at a junction of driveways just beyond, with the golf course still to your right. After continuing some distance farther, turn right by a second footpath signpost to pass through a gateway preceding a tree-lined track of earth and gravel. This leads you south west, still alongside the golf course, to a wooden gate leading out on to B3079 at Brook. A few yards right-handed along this, beyond a stream bridge and on your left is The Green Dragon pub, while not much farther along, on your right, is The Bell Inn.

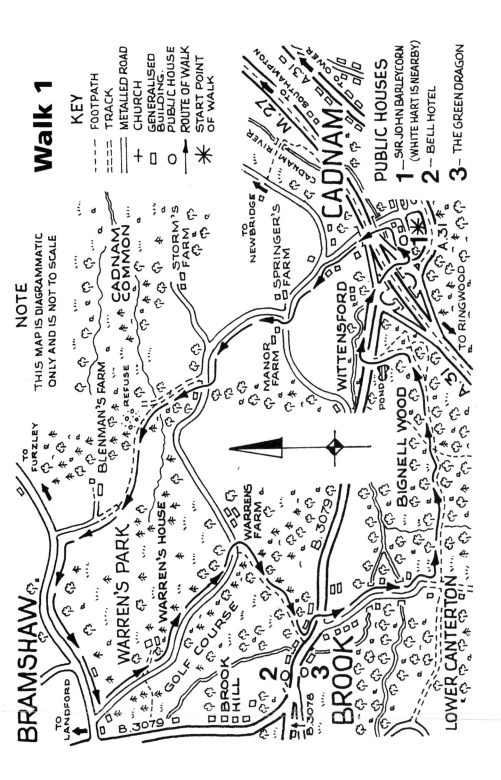

The Sir John Barleycorn, Cadnam

Returning from whichever of these is your choice for mid-walk refreshment, a few yards past where you joined B3079 disregard a narrow lane which turns fairly sharply right and instead fork right, directly beyond, to follow a second narrow lane. Houses alongside this precede two winding woodland brooks, beyond which you briefly ascend to open ground at Lower Canterton, a Forest hamlet, well-hidden from the great wide world without. Disregard a leftward-pointing bridleway sign where the open space starts and carry on for a short distance along what is here a gravel road to where a second bridleway sign, on the left-hand side of the road, points right. Here you turn left to head in precisely the opposite direction on an easterly path through the old oaks, beeches and hollies of Bignell Wood, a beautiful tract of ancient timber where only the sound of A31 traffic through the trees not far to your right intrudes upon a pristine calm that can hardly have changed throughout the centuries. The fallow deer hoofprints that we saw here were of animals whose forebears have ranged these woods since Norman times.

Disregard crossing tracks as you head slightly north of east on a converging course with the ever busy A31. When you reach this, turn left to make your way along a grass clearing, towards the end of which you skirt a shallow pond before emerging on to the unfenced B3079. Follow this road right-handed, under the end of the M27 motorway and so back to Cadnam and your car. The Sir John Barleycorn Inn and The White Hart are not far beyond.

Shady Ways around Woodlands, near Ashurst

WALK 2
Up to 3 hours
5½ miles
Walk begins page 13

Background to the Walk

The Woodlands of today is not conspicuously wooded, being flanked on two sides by low-lying farmland sparsely interspersed with coppices of a size and number which might be expected in any agricultural area. Immediately to the south, though, spreads the New Forest, with woodland extending almost without a break to the outskirts of Lyndhurst and affording plenty of scope for leisurely exploration on foot.

Woodlands is not so much a village in its own right as a residential extension of Netley Marsh. Originally part of the once large parish of Eling, Netley Marsh, including Woodlands, became an independent parish in 1894, at a time when a good deal of building development was taking place in the area. A mere glance at Woodlands today reveals the 19th century origin of much of its housing, strung out as this is along both sides of the road from Netley Marsh and extending south-east along the New Forest's edge towards Ashurst. Apparently at one time there was plenty of thatch in the area, the reedbeds alongside the Test's lower reaches providing an abundant local supply of this material, but you will not see much thatch today. Redbridge, just over the Test where this joins salt water, derives from 'Reedbridge', experts tell us.

Many New Forest placenames are as picturesque as their origin is obscure. A good example is Busketts, the name of a tract of ancient woodland and of a forestry inclosure as well as part of the name of another plantation through which you pass in the

Maps
Landranger 1:50,000
Sheet 196
1:25,000
Outdoor Leisure Map 22,
New Forest
Map reference of Start/Finish
SU324118

How to get there
Follow A3024, Totton's
southern and western bypasses
and A336 to Netley Marsh and
there turn left if approaching
from Southampton, or turn
right if approaching from
Bournemouth by way of
Wessex Way, A338, A31 and
A336 from Cadnam, to follow
the Woodlands-signposted
road. Within half a mile turn
left from this and after a further
very short distance you will
reach The Gamekeeper pub on
your left. Solent Blue
Line/Wilts & Dorset buses on
service 31A between
Southampton, Cadnam and
Lyndhurst pass through
Woodlands by The Gamekeeper.
From Bournemouth and
Ringwood take Solent Blue
Line/Wilts & Dorset service X2
to Netley Marsh and either
change there to service 31A or
walk for about a mile from there
to Woodlands, and the pub.

Pub facilities
The Gamekeeper
Those who remember the Royal
Oak pub at Woodlands of years
gone by will find it now in a
new guise as The Gamekeeper, a

course of this walk — Busketts Lawn Inclosure. Brockishill Inclosure, also on this route, is less mysterious, suggesting, as it does, an ancient haunt of Brock the badger, a well-established New Forest denizen. Brockishill precedes Furzy Lawn Inclosure, about whose meaning again there is no great mystery. Furze, or gorse, occurs abundantly on the more open parts of the Forest. In combination with the word 'lawn', which needs no erudite explanation, it hints at when the wood now so-called had yet to be established on what may well have been much more open ground.

Costicles Inclosure has a more interesting name. Costicles Pond, next door, has been on the map for at least 200 years, during which time it eventually shrank to a half-forgotten wooded swamp, but it has recently been restored with the aid of a conservation grant. Frogs and newts can now breed there again as well as a rare freshwater crustacean, the fairy shrimp, which thrives in ponds which dry out in summer, when it buries itself in the mud while its predators die. The pond pre-existed its namesake inclosure, which is nowadays just a hard-to-distinguish part of a block of plantations with no internal divisions to mark their once separate identities.

Accessible from three sides by busy roads, this tract of timber is a favourite haunt not just of ambitious walkers but of many who merely enjoy a gentle stroll not too far from their cars. Even so, there are quiet corners where you may still get a glimpse of deer. I have seen fallow deer and roe deer here and, once, the fresh tracks of a red deer, so you never know what you might meet around the next corner. I have also seen badgers, though not in the middle hours of the day when most people go walking. These are creatures of the night, which emerge at dusk when all is peaceful.

Winding through the heart of the woods is Bartley Water, a brown, mysterious brook which reaches the sea past Eling tide mill, a working museum open to visitors. At one time this miniature river served as a highway for the otter, a sleek, shy mammal which almost died out in the South but is now doing better

*The Gamekeeper,
Woodlands*

under protection and may eventually make a comeback here. Today the odd heron, perhaps a grey wagtail or two and, in summer, gauzy-winged dragonflies are more likely to be seen if you diverge to follow the brook on its serpentine twistings among the trees.

Walk 2

Distance: *Allow 3 hours for a walk of five-and-a-half miles.*
Leaving the Gamekeeper pub at Woodlands behind you on your right, follow the cottage-flanked road for a very short distance to a brick-parapeted stream bridge flanked by a footpath sign. Turn left here to cross the first of five stiles with the tree-bordered brook alongside you at first. You follow the right-hand side of three successive small paddocks with intervening stiles to stile number four, beyond which a 3ft wide grass path leads you along a fenced corridor between fields. A plank footbridge and another footbridge with a handrail precede the fifth stile and your point of emergence on to a road.

Follow the road left-handed for a few yards before passing through a metal gate on your left to follow a signposted bridleway: a grassy, tree-bordered track bordered in its turn by meadows bright with buttercups on the spring day when we walked here. A right-hand lily pond with an island was another eyecatching feature. Through a second gate you emerge on to Rossiters Lane, a track which you follow right-handed to emerge on to a metalled road.

Follow this cottage-bordered byway left-handed for a few hundred yards to a leftward bend by Goldenhayes, where you turn right-handed to follow a gravel track signposted as a bridleway. Carry on now to a double gate where a tributary track bends right. A left-hand pedestrian gate precedes a continuation of your own gravel track. Gravel gives way to grass as you continue along a path with a strip of oak woodland on your right and hedged pastureland

Busketts Lawn Inclosure

extending to the Forest edge on your left.

By a metal gate you enter what is officially the New Forest, with a scenic transformation at once immediate and spectacular. You now follow the right-hand edge of some picturesque ancient wood-land, with cottages to your right. Beyond a vehicle barrier a gravel road leads on ahead, with fenced woodland to your left. A driveway between this wood and the Forest's edge precedes a road which you follow left-handed through open forest to a left-hand gate where you enter Brockishill Inclosure. This fenced plantation was one of many created in the mid-19th century following the passing of an Act of Parliament designed to end the New Forest's days as a royal hunting ground. This measure, the Deer Removal Act of 1851, was only partially successful in achieving the aim embodied in its title, but very much more so in its allied purpose of enabling the Crown to fence off and plant up thousands of extra acres of once open Forest for growing timber. Brockishill Inclosure thus came into being in 1860.

Beech, oak and pine flank the gravel road you now follow south. Just over half-a-mile ahead, after a brook, Bartley Water, you enter Furzy Lawn Inclosure. At the next track crossing you turn left to head east, soon leaving the inclosure by way of a double gate, the left-hand one of which is for pedestrians. You now follow a well-defined track through open forest. Within a matter of yards you cross a stream culvert just beyond which you keep right where a subsidiary track bears left and continue through old woodland of oak and beech to an open grassy area where tall pines are in view on the far side at the western end of the next inclosure.

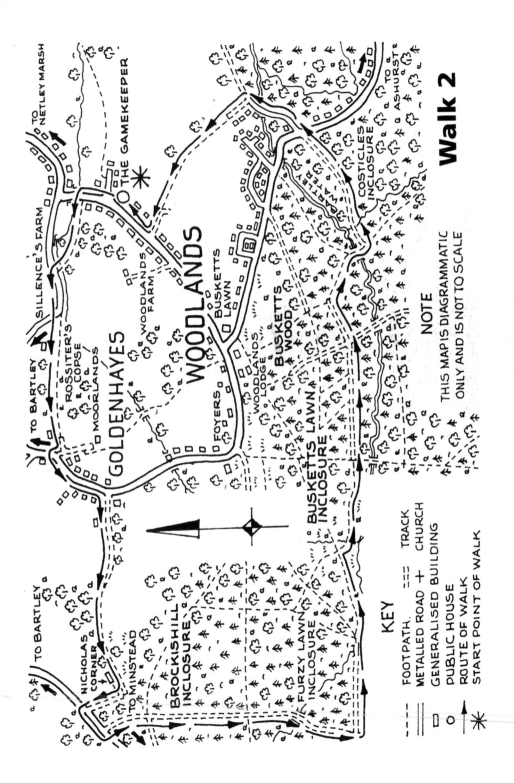

Walk 2

NOTE

THIS MAP IS DIAGRAMMATIC
ONLY AND IS NOT TO SCALE

KEY

--- FOOTPATH.   === TRACK
▭ METALLED ROAD   ✝ CHURCH
GENERALISED BUILDING
◻ PUBLIC HOUSE
○ ROUTE OF WALK
✳ START POINT OF WALK

GOLDENHAYES

WOODLANDS

BUSKETTS
LAWN

BUSKETTS
LAWN
INCLOSURE

BUSKETTS
WOOD

WOODLANDS
LODGE

FOYERS

WOODLANDS
FARM

ROSSITER'S
COPSE

MOORLANDS

SILLENCE'S FARM

THE GAMEKEEPER

COSTICLES
INCLOSURE

MATLEY WOOD

BROCKISHILL
INCLOSURE

FURZY LAWN
INCLOSURE

NICHOLAS
CORNER

TO MINSTEAD

TO BARTLEY

TO BARTLEY

TO NETLEY MARSH

TO ASHURST

A footbridge over the Bartley Water

Carry on ahead across the open ground until you are parallel with a clump of oaks on the clearing's edge to your left, where you join and follow diagonally right an ill-defined, wheel-rutted track. After crossing a shallow drain in a slight declivity this track ascends into primeval-looking old timber through which it approaches coniferous Busketts Lawn Inclosure. You enter this plantation by a double gate, of which the right-hand one in this case is for walkers, and follow a grass ride ahead. This brings you quickly to a track crossing where you join and follow ahead a gravel forestry road between tall pines and groves of oak.

At the next gravel road intersection the easterly road you are following bends slightly left, and then soon swings right to cross a scenic stretch of the Bartley Water by a fairly deep ford, parallel with which is a substantial wooden footbridge. Trees here create a perpetual gloaming which enhances the rivulet's mystery as it twists and turns among them. Take the next left-turning gravel road through the mixed broadleafed trees and conifers of Costicles Inclosure.

Another double gate, the left-hand one being for pedestrian use, marks the point where you leave the New Forest. Cross a metalled road ahead, turning left and then right to follow Fletchwood Lane. This is macadamised as far as a bridge where you recross Bartley Water. A bridleway sign points ahead here. With privately-owned Fletchwood Copse to your right, follow a gravel road ahead to the far end of some bungalows, where a gravel drive leads you left-handed past more bungalows to a stile flanked by a footpath sign. Cross this to follow a hedged grass path between pastures towards Woodlands, directly ahead. Reaching the road here, follow it right-handed back to The Gamekeeper and your car.

Pinewoods and Heather near Hardley

WALK 3
Up to 3 hours
4½ miles
Walk begins page 19

Background to the Walk

Perhaps surprisingly for so small a place in relation to the sizeable modern communities around it, Hardley has a history dating back to Norman times, when it rated a mention as 'Hardelie' in the Domesday survey. This derives from the Old English 'heard' and 'leah', meaning 'hard clearing' and therefore suggesting an island of human settlement amid surrounding wooded or waste land.

Hardley today is an industrial appendage of the lower Waterside area under the shadow of Fawley Refinery and is the first place you reach after skirting the New Forest by way of the busy A326. It links up in turn with Holbury, only a little way beyond which is populous Blackfield. Both of these last two places are modern developments largely created to accommodate those employed at the refinery and in the rash of satellite industries that have sprung up around the area, while Fawley itself retains at least something of the rural charm and atmosphere of times past.

The whole area was remote and inaccessible until the early years of the 20th century, when there was talk of constructing a railway — possibly to include access to the Isle of Wight by way of a tunnel under the Solent. There is a tradition that a causeway once existed between Lepe, on the Solent shore, and the Island opposite, this supposedly having been served by a Roman road from Eling — a road so named at Dibden Purlieu runs parallel with A326 and earthwork vestiges elsewhere correspond with the course of an ancient highway.

The railway idea was initially shelved in favour of a

Maps
Landranger 1:50,000
Sheet 196
1:25,000
Outdoor Leisure Map 22, New Forest
Map Reference of Start/Finish
SU429049

How to get there
The pub at Hardley nowadays called Hogshead in the Forest lies on the left-hand side of A326, the Totton-Fawley road, a few yards in the Fawley direction as you approach from Hardley roundabout. To reach A326 from Southampton follow A3024 west out of the city and then A35 to the far end of Totton's southern bypass and there turn left. From the Bournemouth direction follow A35 and A337 via Christchurch to Lymington, and B3054 from there, bypassing Beaulieu village centre en route to Dibden Purlieu roundabout, where you join and follow right-handed A326 for nearly 2 miles. Take the third exit from the next roundabout, at Hardley, to reach Hogshead in the Forest on your left. Solent Blue Line buses on services 38 and X9 from Southampton, Totton and Hythe (service 36 from Hythe on Sundays) pass through Hardley en route to Langley, Fawley or Calshot. Wilts & Dorset buses on services 121, 122, 123 and 124 from Bournemouth connect at

Lymington with service 112 to Hythe, where a change should be made to Solent Blue Line service X9 or 38 (service 36 on Sundays) for Hardley.

Pub facilities
Hogshead in the Forest
Previously known as The Forest Home, this pub just beyond the roundabout where the A326 is joined by the old road from Hythe to Blackfield and Fawley is only a very short walk from the Forest, with which its links are reinforced by its present name. Open from 1100-1430 and 1630-2300 from Mondays to Thursdays, all day from 1100-2300 on Fridays and Saturdays and from 1200-2230 on Sundays, the pub, a Whitbread house, enjoys a busy lunchtime trade serving local industry and is a popular place of call at both lunchtimes and evenings for people from near and far. Real ales regularly available here are Flower's Original and Wadworth 6X. Also on draught are Whitbread Best Bitter, Boddington's Creamflow, Guinness, Murphy's Irish stout, Heineken, Heineken Export and Stella lagers and Strongbow dry cider. Food may be ordered between 1200-1430 and 1900-2100 except on Sundays, when food is available between 1200-1430 only. There is no formal food menu, dishes of the day being chalked up where all can see what is on offer. Hot pies, sausage dishes and a chef's special are always included, pub policy being to keep prices at a modest level. Traditional bar food listed on a typical day might range from tasty rolls, chips, steak and kidney pie, fish and chips and scampi and chips to barbecue chicken, burgers, pasta, rump steak platter and ploughman's, among much else. There is a large garden with a play area

bus service, only to be revived in the 1920s when the oil industry and Fawley first came together. This happened when Anglo Gulf West Indies Petroleum Corporation (AGWI) built a refinery as a source of fuel oil for ships at a time when the big transatlantic liners and others were changing from coal to oil to heat their boilers. Bitumen for road improvements then commencing on an impressive scale was another AGWI product needing rail transport out of Fawley, and so, in the mid-Twenties, a line was at last constructed and opened — and not for refinery purposes only.

Five passenger trains each way on weekdays were soon whittled down to a skeleton service mainly for workmen. This lasted until the mid-Sixties, by which time Esso had taken over and hugely expanded Fawley Refinery. With its ancillary enterprises this now occupies most of what used to be Cadland Park, seat of the Drummond family from the 18th century onwards. Drummonds still own much land in the area, their home, the present Cadland House, being located close to the shore between Calshot and Lepe.

Apart from where it starts and finishes this is a Forest walk throughout, traversing formerly open heathland, part of which has been planted with trees. This came about following the New Forest Act of 1949, which made provision for the enclosure of additional acres of open land for timber production. These are known as Verderers' Inclosures from the fact that they could only be made with the approval of the New Forest Court of Verderers after careful consideration of proposals by the Forestry Commission in each individual case. Most of the eleven new plantations which resulted act as visual buffers between industry, busy roads and the like and the heartland of the Forest, as in the case of Fawley and Dibden Inclosures, traversed on this walk.

The open heath which remains, with its heather, gorse and scattered seedling pines, is a wilderness plateau grazed by ponies, affording habitat to the rare Dartford warbler and a few other birds, and inspiring widely differing reactions from different observers. In his *Rural Rides*, William Cobbett railed against its

The Hogshead in the Forest, Hardley

for children, who are not allowed in the bars, nor are dogs. Walkers with muddy boots are welcome to use the public bar, and followers of this walk may leave their cars in the large pub car park. Pool, darts and electronic pub games are complemented by occasional live entertainment and there is a log fire in the winter. The telephone number is 01703 842270.

hostile, unproductive emptiness, which he likened to what he regarded as the ultimate in rural uselessness, Bagshot Heath in Surrey. In our overcrowded modern world one learns to appreciate such empty spaces as still remain for what they are, and Beaulieu Heath is one such space.

Walk 3

Distance: *Allow up to 3 hours for this four-and-a-half mile walk.*
From Hogshead in the Forest cross the road to follow a signposted footpath which begins directly opposite the pub car park, by way of a cul-de-sac called Roman Road. The entrance to the footpath proper is flanked by industrial premises a very short distance directly ahead. Fenced and tree-bordered at first, the path leads on along the right-hand edge of a pasture with industrial premises to your right and brings you to another road, which you cross to follow another fenced footpath section. Where you soon reach the end of the industrial complex the path bends at right-angles to your right, with industry still to the right of it. A landfill site lies to your left as you approach a tree-shaded wooden gate with pedestrian access alongside.

Here you enter the New Forest, passing straight from peripheral industry to a land of peace and ponies, not to mention other walkers and local workers jogging during their lunch-break. Beyond the gate a well-defined footpath bears half-left towards the pines of Fawley Inclosure, which earlier formed a backdrop to the view across the landfill site. Long-needled Corsican pine and heather are the main features of this plantation, where the ground had to be ploughed to create a ridge-and-furrow base before trees could be successfully planted. You can still see where this was done as you proceed towards a point where the trees open out to present a view across a valley where a stream has broadened into a miniature lake.

On your way towards this you cross what the map shows as a linear earthwork running from north-west to south-east and pointing, in the latter direction, in a straight line towards Lepe. This is where the Roman road ended that was supposed to be linked with a ford making it possible to cross the Solent on foot when the tide was low, though it has to be said that there is not a shred of proof to back up this notion.

In the valley below the miniature lake, which is really no more than a pool, you cross Dark Water stream by a wooden footbridge — Hardley Bridge. A few yards ahead, uphill, you reach the end of Fawley Inclosure and the beginning of Beaulieu Heath proper. Tracks divide here, with the right-hand one re-entering the wood. You keep left-ahead to pass through a former gateway and follow a track that at first hugs the edge of Fawley Inclosure and then gradually veers away to the left of it, heading due west in an arrow-straight line across the heath.

Heather, gorse and the occasional stunted pine are virtually all that grow on this gravelly tableland. Apart from the odd, drab meadow pipit and a passing crow or two, bird-life is scarce in these surroundings, though the heath is home to at least one rarity. I remember being taken here with my wife many years ago to see my very first Dartford warbler. This long-tailed, little brown bird derives its popular name, 'fuzz-topper', from its habit of perching briefly atop a gorse bush before slipping away from view amid the prickles underneath in search of the spiders and other small prey upon which it subsists. Almost wiped out by severe winters in 1947 and 1963, this resident warbler has since recovered and re-established itself more securely on a handful of southern heathlands in the New Forest and elsewhere.

Ahead you will see traffic on the road between Hythe and Beaulieu as you strike west to follow the track across the heath. In case you should wonder why such a track exists, the reason becomes apparent once you cross the Beaulieu road, where a marker identifies the route followed by a gas pipeline from Fawley, buried underneath the gravel. Having crossed the road, carry on to a diagonal crossing of tracks about halfway between the road and the edge of woodland left-ahead. Bear right here and head north-west to the next track intersection. No fewer than six different tracks converge here. Take one which bears half-right to skirt the right-hand end of a small birchwood to cross a heathery dip and reach an open gateway at the southern end of Dibden Inclosure.

A twin to Fawley Inclosure in both origin and character, like its sibling it is no longer, strictly speaking, an inclosure. Trees having grown beyond the stage where browsing ponies can do much mischief, commoners' animals can now share this wood with the many local people and others who use it to walk their dogs, thanks to the facility of a car park.

Follow a gravel road ahead between pure pinewoods where both the Scots and the Corsican species may be found. Every so often grassy side paths

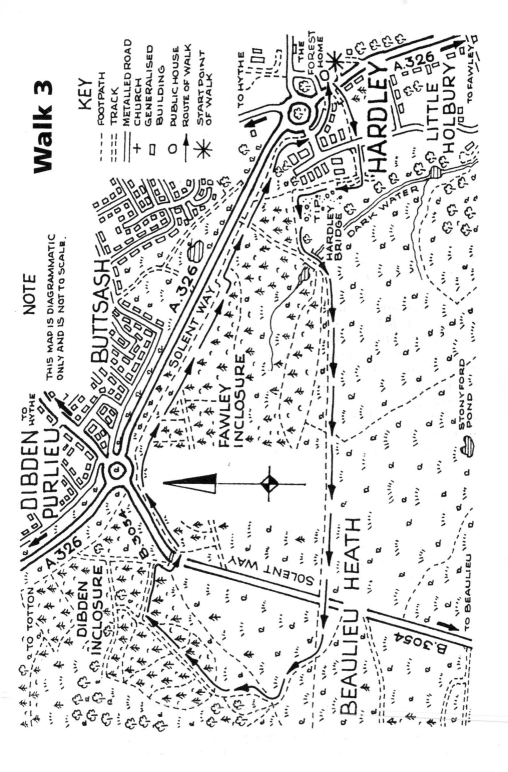

Hardley Bridge

penetrate the conifer gloom. For present purposes disregard them. At the first ride intersection your gravelled way angles slightly right. Continue along it to a meeting point of five tracks in the woodland centre. Take the third exit to follow the main gravel road right-handed. A gate which is normally padlocked but with a pedestrian access adjoining precedes a car park and a second, open, gateway through which you emerge to reach the Hythe to Beaulieu road. Follow this right-handed through a gateway alongside a cattlegrid and then cross the road and follow left-handed a section of The Solent Way long distance walking route from Milford-on-Sea to Emsworth.

This is obliged by the lack of a continuous coastal footpath to head inland and even to follow roads along parts of its course, although efforts to remedy this situation have not been lacking and may yet produce results.

Here the Solent Way's route runs parallel with the Beaulieu road, on your left, with Fawley Inclosure on your right. Within a very short distance of Dibden Purlieu roundabout the woodland-edge clearing you are now following bends at right-angles to the right and is shared by ponies with pylons and power-lines. Follow a fairly well-defined path close to the left-hand side of the clearing. After bridging a stream the main path bears half-right into Fawley Inclosure but a subsidiary path continues along the left-hand side of the clearing. Where another path later angles right, again you continue left-ahead to a gateway where you leave the New Forest. A tree-bordered bridleway leads ahead to a metalled road, after crossing which you follow a metalled road ahead to where a gravel cul-de-sac bends left, with a bridleway exit on to A326 opposite the pub where you started.

Fields, Woods and Shore near Langley and Exbury

WALK 4
4 or 5 hours
6½ or 8 miles
Walk begins page 24

Background to the Walk

Between the New Forest and Southampton Water's western shoreline there was once a strip of quiet countryside largely forgotten by the outside world. Marchwood was unfeignedly rural, Hythe was an old world fishing village linked by ferry with Southampton but otherwise difficult of access, and Fawley was a byword for rustic remoteness and seclusion.

Then came a whole host of changes in the course of a few decades — aviation to Calshot, oil importation to Fawley, power boats to Hythe and much, much else that was destined to alter the face of the Waterside area virtually beyond recognition.

Yet this is not quite the whole story. On either side of Marchwood there are still green fields and leafy woods. Saltmarshes and remnants of inland verdure survive on the Fawley side of Hythe — and beyond now-populous Blackfield and neighbouring Langley you can still be right in the heart of the country as soon as you step off the metalled roads.

Earthwork traces of a road built by the Romans may still be seen just south of Langley. This road led to the shore at Lepe, from which a causeway to the Isle of Wight is supposed to have existed, though this is perhaps just a colourful legend. A more recent local link with history is the fact that Langley Lodge was a childhood home of Lawrence of Arabia. The house no longer exists.

Exbury is a rare surviving example of an estate village still largely populated by estate workers and their families, insulated by woods and water from other

Maps
*Landranger 1:50,000
Sheet 196
1:25,000
Leisure 22, New Forest
Map reference of Start/Finish
SU447011*

How to get there
From Southampton head west along A3024 and A35 to the western end of Totton's southern bypass and turn left here to follow A326 to reach Hardley and Holbury, at the far end of which bear right-ahead for Blackfield, through which you continue ahead to adjoining Langley, where The Langley Tavern is on your right. From Bournemouth follow Wessex Way, eastbound A35 and A337 to Lymington, B3054 to Hilltop crossroads a mile beyond Beaulieu, and here bear right to follow the Fawley road. At the next crossroads after skirting Holbury, turn right at traffic lights for Blackfield and Langley, where The Langley Tavern is on your right. From Southampton Solent Blue Line buses on services X9 and 38 either terminate at Langley, continue through it to Lepe Beach in summer, or bypass it at Blackfield en route to Fawley and Calshot (Blackfield is almost a mile from Langley). Wilts & Dorset buses on service 121, 122, 123 and 124 from Bournemouth connect at Lymington with service 112 to

Hythe, where a change should be made to Solent Blue Line buses on services 38 or X9 for Langley or Blackfield.

Pub facilities
The Langley Tavern
Built just before World War II on the site of a previous hostelry, this combines normal pub amenities with en-suite bed and breakfast accommodation, including colour TV in each bedroom. A good choice of brews including Wadworth 6X, Chiswick Bitter and Boddington's real ales as well as Whitbread Best Bitter and Mild are complemented by a wide-ranging bar menu made possible by recently upgraded kitchen facilities. Menus are changed periodically but typically include six different kinds of sandwiches, soup of the day, prawn cocktail served with brown bread and butter, deep fried mushrooms with garlic mayonnaise, jumbo jackets served with salad garnish and four different ploughman's. Main meals typically include scampi served in a basket with chips, jumbo sausage and chips served in a basket, chicken portion with chips, American burger with salad and chips, deep fried cod or plaice fillet with lemon wedge and chips, home-made lasagne with salad, home-made steak and kidney pie with peas and a choice of potato, and a home-made vegetarian dish of the day. A good choice of steaks and grills at very reasonable prices is another popular feature, while sweets are likely to include sticky toffee cream, lemon meringue pie and death by chocolate, all served with cream. Traditional roasts are a Sunday lunchtime speciality. The garden includes a children's play area with a bouncy castle, swings, trampolines and an animal

centres of population and there is every reason to hope it will so remain: an oasis of peace in a troubled world.

Exbury, it seems, is a corruption of Teocreberie, the name by which the locality was recorded in the Domesday Survey. In times gone by the neighbouring Beaulieu River was sometimes known as the Exe, this being a Celtic term meaning 'the water', though if there is a link, as one might have thought, with the name of Exbury, the placename pundits do not say so.

The village used to be where Lower Exbury now is, a mile from its present location and right at the mouth of the Beaulieu River. The estate was owned by the Mitford family when, in the early 19th century, lord of the manor William Mitford decided to move the village, lock, stock and barrel, to where it is now. New cottages of the local yellow brick were built for his workers. The new church that was also built made use of similar materials plus some stonework from the mediaeval chapel at Lower Exbury. Later sheathed in Isle of Wight stone, the modern church contains memorials to members of another landowning family — Lord Forster of Lepe, a 1920s Governor General of Australia, and two of his sons, who died as a result of wounds sustained in World War I.

Lord Forster lived at Inchmery, within yards of the Solent shore. Next on the scene as a major landowner was Lionel Nathan de Rothschild, of the well known banking family, who first bought property locally in 1912. An inheritance in 1916 enabled him to purchase Exbury itself, where after the First World War he set to work to transform 250 acres of tangled woodlands into a rhododendron paradise which has won worldwide renown. Edmund de Rothschild, Lionel's son, now runs the family property, his own son Nicholas also being involved in the care of the famous gardens, which are visited and admired by scores of thousands every year.

Walk 4

Distance: *Allow 4 hours for the six-and-a-half mile walk or 5 hours for the eight mile walk.*
Directly north of The Langley Tavern turn left to follow a driveway which becomes a fenced and tree-

The Langley Tavern

corner among other attractions. Petanque, pool and darts are played. On Sunday evenings there is occasional live entertainment, and Sunday quizzes are popular. Pub-using walkers may use the pub car park. The pub is open all day, from 1100-2300 on weekdays and 1200-2230 on Sundays. Food may be ordered between 1200-1400 (roasts only on Sunday lunchtimes) and 1900-2200. The telephone number is 01703 891402.

lined path leading into another road which you follow left-ahead. At a fork of no-through-roads bear left to follow an unadopted road. Beyond bordering houses this becomes a gravelly path which dips between trees to cross by a handrailed footbridge Dark Water brook, itself tree-shaded. The path then rises to pass between oak woodland and pastures margined by trees, soon dipping again before emerging on to a road.

Follow this road right-handed with a field on your left at first, followed by a wood, just past the start of which you enter it over a stile. A well-defined path now leads you south-westward through oaks and hazels which dip right-handed into a parallel stream valley, while farmland remains visible through trees on your left-hand side. Your path fairly soon joins a track leading to buildings on your right which you follow ahead, out of the wood, towards a high-fenced garden on the outskirts of Exbury. Just short of the fence your path bends left to the end of the garden, where it bends right to join a road serving a residential area. Follow this road left-handed to a T-junction with a lane, which you follow right-handed.

This leads past cottages to a T-junction in Exbury village centre, where you turn right, past the entrance to the estate office and yard on your left. Exbury's Church of St Katharine lies just back from the road, on your right.

If you are energetic, you can extend the six-and-a-half-mile walk to one of about eight miles by continuing north along the road past the second of two lodge cottages on your left, then turning left — not through the wrought-iron gates, which mark the start of a private driveway to Exbury House, but to follow a very narrow metalled lane a few yards farther on. This leads between grassy acres followed by oaks and rhododendrons, passing under an ornate arch between two parts of Exbury Gardens and then descending through more boscage. Dwellings face the lane from your right as you approach the private entrance to a boatyard at Gilbury Hard. A signposted footpath here turns right to emerge through trees on to the bank of the winding Beaulieu River estuary, a placid waterway best arrived at when high tide is lapping the saltings, with woods and water close together as you look along its course.

Head back the same way to Exbury village, passing the church now on your left (or turn back from it if you omitted the side-excursion to Gilbury Hard) and keep right-ahead at the village centre road junction just beyond. Signposted to Inchmery, the lane you now follow is flanked on your right by parkland and then farmland on both sides. Not very far along it, a footpath sign and a stile on your left precede a path across a field, beyond which the Solent gleams to your right.

You soon enter a wood through which you follow a right-bending ride, the public footpath being waymarked at various subsequent ride turnings. This involves a right-angled turn left to follow a ride which rises to reach the east end of the wood. At a signposted junction of paths here you turn right to follow the wood edge. After fairly soon passing through an opening at the right-hand end of a hedge between two fields your path continues alongside the wood, as appropriate waymarking makes clear.

Two successive footpath signposts indicate right-hand turns of the path, the well-used course of which is self-evident as it leads back into the wood, twice dipping to cross streams by plank bridges before eventually angling left between lines of trees to a kissing-gate. A few yards beyond this your path, whose course is clearly waymarked throughout its length, emerges on to a lane which you follow left-handed for a short distance to the Solent shore at Inchmery. Here a stile with a footpath sign marks the start of a path along the shore which we found under water at high tide. After a pause for a picnic lunch we therefore continued along the shore road. Oak trees leaning out over the water precede the grounds of Inchmery House and a junction of lanes where we turned right to follow a signposted fenced path leading through trees back to the shore, along which a gravelly path continues trending leftward.

On a later visit at low tide I followed the shore path east from Inchmery, picking my way around the debris of cliff erosion at some points but finding the going quite easy. A myriad oozy crenellations carve up the saltmarsh to the right here, where the Beaulieu River's outflow reaches the Solent after sweeping around Gull Island, part of North Solent National Nature Reserve and a breeding place for large numbers of gulls and other sea birds.

Coast protection work has been carried out alongside the all-states-of-the-tide path which takes you east past Lepe House to where a concrete path diverges left and climbs to the parallel road. Follow the road left-handed to where it shortly bends left and at this point cross a stile flanked by a footpath sign on your right. A well-defined grassy farm track leads you right-handed, soon curving left to cross a marshy area before rising to reach a gateway flanked by a stile. Beyond this your path bears half-left from the wheel-rutted farm track and climbs to a tree-lined field boundary, where a stile precedes a path leading

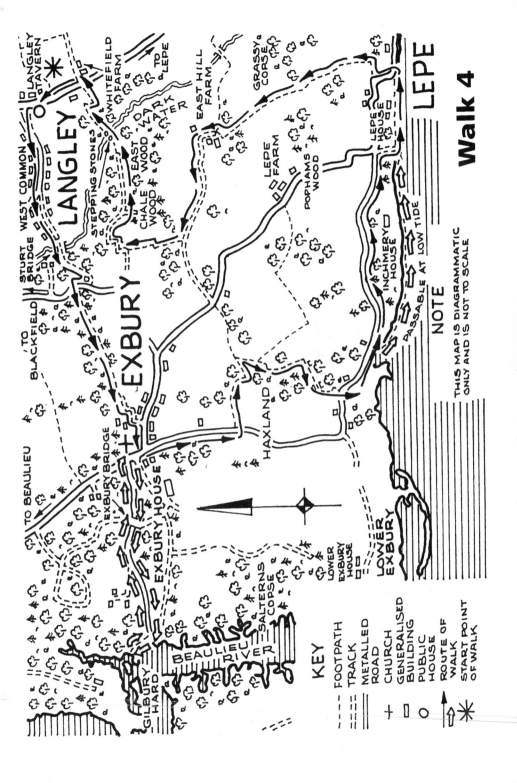

Walk 4

LEPE

LANGLEY

EXBURY

LANGLEY TAVERN

WEST COMMON

STURT BRIDGE

TO BLACKFIELD

STEPPING STONES

WHITEFIELD FARM

TO LEPE

EAST WOOD DARK WATER

CHALE WOOD

EAST HILL FARM

GRASSY CORSE

LEPE FARM

POPHAMS WOOD

LEPE HOUSE

INCHMERY HOUSE

PASSABLE AT LOW TIDE

HAXLAND

EXBURY BRIDGE

EXBURY HOUSE

TO BEAULIEU

LOWER EXBURY HOUSE

LOWER EXBURY

SALTERNS CORSE

GILBURY HARD

BEAULIEU RIVER

NOTE

THIS MAP IS DIAGRAMMATIC ONLY AND IS NOT TO SCALE

KEY

- – – – – FOOTPATH
- ┄┄┄┄ TRACK
- ═══ METALLED ROAD
- ✝ CHURCH
- ▢ GENERALISED BUILDING
- ○ PUBLIC HOUSE
- ⇧ ROUTE OF WALK
- ✳ START POINT OF WALK

The Solent Shore path at Lepe

directly across a large field to skirt the left-hand end of some woodland before continuing straight on to the field's far side.

Be prepared for muddy going if the weather has been wet as you carry on across the next large field on the same footpath alignment, heading for a stile on the field's far side. The path here is sometimes scored by deep wheel ruts from heavy farm machinery.

Take a last look back across farmland to the sea through a frame of trees before following a green ride through the wood that now lies ahead. After crossing a shallow stream you head uphill to skirt right-handed of farm buildings at East Hill Farm, where you join a bridleway which you follow left-handed. A gravelly road now leads you through farmland, with a wood in view to your right.

The wood and the gravel road converge, and where the road-cum-bridleway bears left you pass through a waymarked gateway on your right to follow a fairly wide woodland ride which angles leftward. At the wood end bear slightly right to join and follow a fenced grassy track, with trees to your right, along the right-hand edge of a field to reach a T-junction with a green lane. Follow this grassy lane right-handed along a twisty course into a wood, soon after entering which you disregard a right-forking track as well as subsequent minor tracks and paths diverging to right and left.

A stepped and handrailed section of your well-used public footpath presently descends to concrete block stepping-stones over Dark Water brook, beyond which you climb to follow a gravelly path to a stile and a stream footbridge which you cross. Leaving the wood by another stile, your path angles right to skirt a paddock before crossing a further stile and following a fenced leftward course to a final stile. Here you emerge opposite Whitefield Farm on the Lepe side of Langley. Follow the road you join here left-handed for a few hundred yards to arrive back at The Langley Tavern.

Through Riverside Woods to Bucklers Hard

WALK 5
At least 3 hours
5 miles
Walk begins page 32

Background to the Walk

Beaulieu, so aptly named 'beautiful place', has been a focal point of attraction for outsiders throughout the centuries. Early Norman kings had a hunting lodge here which was known as 'Bellus Locus'. Then, when King John decided to make his peace with the Cistercian monks, he gave them Beaulieu and its surrounding lands for their Abbey of St Mary de Bella Loco Regis.

The abbey, we learn, took 40 years to build and attained a size comparable with that of Winchester Cathedral. The community supported itself by the produce of farms and allied enterprises scattered about an extensive estate stretching down to the Solent. Starting in 1204, the Cistercian era ended when Henry VIII dissolved monastic institutions everywhere and confiscated their lands. Thus in 1538 an ancestor of the present Lord Montagu acquired the property.

The village of Beaulieu probably began as a cluster of cottages built to accommodate the large labour force required to construct the abbey. The original dwellings would have been of mud or wattle-and-daub, the traditional domestic building materials of the area. From the 17th century onwards these were superseded by houses built of locally-made bricks. Many from that period still survive in Beaulieu High Street. Palace House is on part of the site of the old abbey, as is the parish Church of St Mary. Between the abbey remains and the village winds the picturesque Beaulieu River, tidal upstream as far as the bridge. This bridge dates back to the 13th century and was

Maps
Landranger 1:50,000
Sheet 196
1:25,000
Outdoor Leisure 22, New Forest
Map Reference of Start/Finish
SU386022

How to get there
Beaulieu lies at the junction of B3056 from Lyndhurst and B3054 from Lymington and Dibden Purlieu roundabout, nr Hythe, reached from Southampton via A3024 and A35 to the western end of Totton's southern bypass and from there via A326. At Dibden Purlieu roundabout turn right for Beaulieu. Lymington is reached from Bournemouth via A35 to the eastern end of Christchurch bypass and then via A337 by way of Highcliffe and the outskirts of New Milton. Beaulieu can be reached direct from Lymington via B3054 and from Brockenhurst via B3055 to Hatchet pond, and then via B3054. The public car park in Beaulieu lies in the triangle enclosed by B3056, B3054 and Beaulieu High Street. Solent Blue Line services X9 and 38 from Southampton connect at Hythe with Wilts & Dorset service 112 to Beaulieu, and on summer Sundays with Solent Blue Line service 34, which runs to Beaulieu. Wilts & Dorset bus services 121, 122, 123 and 124 from

Bournemouth connect at
Lymington with service 112 to
Beaulieu, and on summer
Sundays there is one bus each
way on service 123 between
Bournemouth and the Motor
Museum at Beaulieu.

Pub facilities
Monty's, Beaulieu

*Open between 1100-1500 and
1800-2300 from Mondays to
Fridays, from 1100–2300 on
Saturdays and from 1200-2230
on Sundays, Monty's, formerly
The Wine Press and before that
Spats Bar, is a section of the
old-established Montagu Arms
Hotel which has been
transformed into a pub serving
brasserie-style food direct from
the hotel kitchen. In keeping
with its character, Monty's has
been extensively altered and
refurbished to enhance its
village pub atmosphere.
Carpets have been removed and
there is now an exposed wooden
floor as well as much pleasing
new stonework and handsome
wood panelling. A fireplace has
been restored to use, with a log
fire warming the bar in winter,
and the tables and chairs are
new. Real ales on draught here
are the popular Ringwood
Forty-Niner and True Glory,
and an exceptionally good
range of white and red wines is
available by the bottle or served
by the glass. Main meals
include such dishes as slow-
cooked knuckle of lamb served
with creamy potatoes and either
a side salad or green beans,
rump steak with French fries,
tomatoes and mushrooms,
sausages served with an onion
gravy and mash, and flash fried
haddock with tomato and
shallot salad, basil oil and a
poached egg. Classic spaghetti
Bolognese, salmon and broccoli
linguini and a tempting
selection of burgers,
Continental-style salads, Cajun
chicken, snacks and beverages*

The Montagu Arms, Beaulieu

built of quarry-stone by the monks. It made a
convenient site for a tide mill which functioned well
into the 20th century, having been brought back into
temporary use during World War II after earlier
closure.

The National Motor Museum was founded and
developed as a tribute to the marvels of the internal
combustion engine by the present Lord Montagu,
whose father was one of the pioneers of motoring,
having been involved, among much else, with
persuading Parliament to allow cars to be driven
faster than the once legal limit of 12 mph!

Wheels do not reign unchallenged at Beaulieu.
New Forest ponies and donkeys wander at will about
the village, though this has not always been the case.
Where the Forest proper ends and the Beaulieu
Manor estate begins the roads were once gated, and I
can just remember a time when these gates were
opened by estate staff for every individual car or
other item of wheeled traffic, being closed again
afterwards to help keep livestock where it belonged,
on the open Forest.

Access to alcoholic refreshment has rarely been
lacking in this community. The monks made wine
from their own vineyards, while the village itself in
later years was well supplied with pubs. At one time

The Beaulieu River near Bucklers Hard

are among other items on Monty's bar menu. Food may be ordered between 1200-1430 and 1800-2130 seven days a week.

The Yachtsman's Bar and Galley, Bucklers Hard
This forms part of the Master Builder's House Hotel, which preserves much of the atmosphere of the time when master shipbuilder Henry Adams lived here. Hours of opening are flexible: 1100-2300 on fine summer weekdays with plenty of visitors around and from 1200-2230 on similar Sundays, but closing from 1500 to 1900 at other times. Courage Best and Directors real ales are on draught as well as John Smith's Bitter, Strongbow cider, Guinness and Foster's, and Kronenbourg lagers. To the rear of the bar is a secluded beer garden where you can relax in the sunshine or cool off in the shade while enjoying your favourite brew and refreshing yourself for the walk back to Beaulieu, or you can walk through to The Galley and sample something from a menu ranging from casseroles, fish and lasagne to soups, salads and ploughman's. Basic food ordering times are 1200-1400 and 1900-2100, subject to seasonal variations, weather conditions and visitor demand, waitress service being provided.

there were five of these. The sole survivor is The Montagu Arms, so-named since 1742 when what had previously been The George, and before that The Ship, identified itself with the owning family. Today a substantial hotel, this was once a modest village hostelry and the scene of an annual fair dating from 1607. About 100 years ago the first Lord Montagu put an end to this because of drunkenness and riotous behaviour by some who attended.

Bailey's Hard, on the route of this walk, was a local centre for brickmaking and still possesses a Brickyard Cottage. The term 'hard' crops up in several place-names locally and refers to the presence of firm, hard access to salt water over otherwise treacherous mud.

Bucklers Hard is thought to have taken its name from a local family called Buckle. It started life as 'Montagu's Town', the second Duke of Montagu having envisaged it as an English base for the West Indian trade from St. Lucia, his island property. It became, instead, a shipbuilding centre. Between 1698 and 1818 no fewer than 60 vessels were launched here, including a number of men-of-war whose names became famous in England's naval confrontation with Napoleon. The *Agamemnon*, Nelson's favourite, was one of these. New Forest oak was a prime material for building these great ships, and a man who supervised their construction was master builder Henry Adams, whose home is now an hotel. There is a Henry Adams Room where a representation of the great man himself may be seen poring over architectural drawings, while in the Maritime Museum the local world over which he held sway is highlighted for visitors to appreciate.

Bucklers Hard's twin terraces of dwellings flank a scenic descent to the river and look today much as they did when the 'wooden walls' were being erected. The whole village is preserved in such a way that, strolling through it, you feel you are walking back in time to the 18th century, its heyday. While some of the cottages are still lived in, others are presented as time capsules complete with contents just as they were 200 years and more ago — the erstwhile New Inn, the Shipwright's Cottage and a labourer's cottage among them.

Walk 5

Distance: *Allow at least 3 hours for this five mile walk.*
From Beaulieu's public car park take the pedestrian exit to the High Street, which you cross to follow a signposted gravel footpath between dwellings and around a double bend. Back gardens flank your approach to a playing field, which you cross to a stile of the walk-through type preceding a gravel road, which you follow right-handed. Just ahead of you now is a gate bypassed by another walk-through stile, beyond which the fenced gravel road-cum-footpath carries on between spreading pastures, with the wood-bordered Beaulieu River curving away from your view on the left.

After walking around a cattlegrid you continue to where a muddy, tree-shaded creek wriggles in from the river and edges close to the track you are following along this scenic stretch of the Solent Way, a long-distance walking route which keeps to the coast wherever conditions make this possible. Woodlands crowd close at your point of entry to North Solent National Nature Reserve, which safeguards sensitive wildlife on and around the Beaulieu estuary and the Solent shoreline generally.

Gravel having ceased at the entrance to waste water treatment works a little while previously, the track you now follow emerges from flanking timber to continue along the leftward edge of an arable field, with a line of trees to your left. This brings you through an open gateway directly preceding Bailey's Hard, where Brickyard Cottage, on your left, is a reminder of an industrial activity no longer practised here. At this point you join a gravel road which you follow right-handed. Two other gravel roads join this one from your left until you reach the point, just beyond these, where the signposted public path to Bucklers Hard turns left. A straight gravel track now leads you south-east for nearly a mile through Keeping Copse, where conifer plantations to your right contrast with older oak and beech woodland between yourself and the river estuary, mostly invisible, on your left.

At the far end of Keeping Copse you join and follow right-handed a gravel road, with meadowland on your right and a scrub-bordered estuarine inlet at first on your left, soon followed by Bucklers Hard Yacht Harbour, as the marina

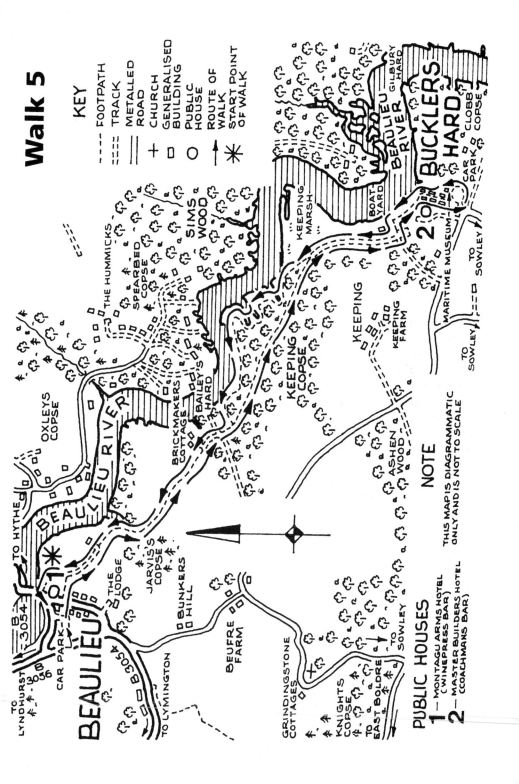

Walk 5

here is called. After crossing the marina's entrance road your path angles slightly left to follow a riverside walk and gravel footpath, bringing you soon to the waterside end of Bucklers Hard's one 'village' street.

Margined generously by grass which is flanked in turn by terraced cottages where time looks to have stood still for these last two centuries, the stony street climbs also past the Master Builder's House Hotel, where the Yachtsman's Bar should be open if the weather is congenial and plenty of visitors are in evidence. At the top of the hill, just round the corner on your left, is Bucklers Hard Maritime Museum, the cost of admission to which includes access to what used to be the New Inn, preserved with all its period features as are two adjoining cottage exhibits representing 18th century Bucklers Hard and the home of a labourer of that era. On the other side of the street is the village shop (still functioning!) and the shipwright's cottage.

That there is no completely different footpath route making possible a circular walk from Beaulieu does little or nothing to discourage the very large numbers of people who choose to sample at least some of this walk, at holiday time especially. You need not return precisely the same way as you came, though. To begin with, follow the riverside walk and the gravel road to which it lead back past the yacht harbour to Keeping Copse. Entering the wood, immediately beyond the car park here fork right from the main gravel path to follow a signposted extension of the earlier riverside walk, a well-defined path which twists and turns in harmony with the serpentine course of the estuary itself, which remains constantly in view through the trees which fringe it, to your right.

The far bank is wooded too, with dense-banked trees punctuated here and there by secluded dwellings of a type and situation which hint at astronomical pricetags and laudatory descriptions in *Country Life*. On your own side trees hem the river without a break for nearly a mile, ensuring many a sheltered corner for waterside wildlife. As well as numerous ducks at various points along the tideline, we surprised a solitary curlew.

After many pleasant meanderings, the riverside walk returns you to the more direct gravelled route, which you follow right-handed to Bailey's Hard. The field-edge path beyond this and the fenced track and road which follow bring you back to the edge of Beaulieu where, instead of recrossing the playing field to reach the High Street and the car park, you can carry on ahead to reach the road right by The Montagu Arms and Monty's Bar. Not many yards past this, up the cobbled High Street, you turn right to re-enter the car park.

A Walk from William Gilpin's Boldre

WALK 6
Allow 3 hours
5 ¼ miles
Walk begins page 37

Background to the Walk

Boldre is a village of the Forest, but not quite in it. The livelihood of those who had their homes here was for centuries linked in various ways with the royal domain on its doorstep. However, not all the means employed by Boldre villagers of the past to help keep body and soul together were calculated to enhance the good of their souls in the Hereafter.

At least, so thought a certain vicar when he arrived in the 1770s to take charge of the local inhabitants' spiritual welfare. The Reverend William Gilpin was appalled by what he saw as the bandit-like habits of Boldre people, much given to poaching and helping themselves to whatever of value they could steal from the wooded wilderness near by. He therefore decided to devote his literary talents to writing books and applying the profits to improving conditions in general for his parishioners. He looked to the Forest for inspiration and found plenty. One of his books in particular, *Remarks on Forest Scenery*, opened the eyes of many to aesthetic rural delights they had hardly noticed until then. It became a classic to rank in importance with a book on natural history by another Hampshire clergyman, the famous Gilbert White of Selborne, at the other end of the county.

Like so many other villages, Boldre today is a quiet place lived in mainly by retired folk and commuters. Yet there is still a sizeable element of those whose links with the soil are not merely ancestral and who could doubtless trace their line back to Gilpin's time.

What is the meaning of the name 'Boldre'? David Mills, in his *Dictionary of English Place-Names*, expresses

Maps
Landranger 1:50,000
Sheet 196
1:25,000
Outdoor Leisure 22, New Forest
Map Reference of Start/Finish
SZ318983

How to get there
The Red Lion at Rope Hill, Boldre is on the south side of the road that heads east through that village from A337 at Battramsley Cross, 2 miles north of Lymington. From Southampton follow A3024 and A35 to Lyndhurst and A337 south from there via Brockenhurst, 3 miles beyond which is Battramsley Cross, where you turn left to follow the road signposted to Boldre and Pilley. From Bournemouth head east along A35 to the eastern end of Christchurch bypass, then follow A337 east via Highcliffe and the southern outskirts of New Milton to Pennington and Lymington, from which you then follow A337 north for 2 miles before turning right at Battramsley Cross for Boldre. Wilts & Dorset buses on service 112 between Hythe, Beaulieu and Lymington pass through Boldre within 100 yards of the pub, and buses on services 56 and 56A between Southampton, Lyndhurst and Lymington connecting there with buses on services 121, 122, 123 and 124 from Bournemouth and

Christchurch, pass the turning for Boldre half-a-mile from The Red Lion.

Pub facilities
The Red Lion, Boldre
Open all day from 1100-2300 on weekdays and from 1200-2230 on Sundays, The Red Lion is an Eldridge Pope house serving Hardy Country Royal Oak and Dorchester Bitter real ales as well as Tetley Keg Bitter, two draught lagers, Guinness and dry cider. It has two bars. There are also a patio and a beer garden where children and dogs are welcome. There is a field at the back of the large rear car park where walkers using the pub may leave their cars. Food can be ordered between 1200-1400 and 1800-2200. The extensive menu includes daily specials ranging from omelettes with prawns, mushrooms, ham or cheese and paupiettes of plaice with prawns to sausages and mash and gammon steak with fried egg. Hot pot of mushrooms with garlic and tomato and smoked salmon platter feature among a choice of ten starters or light snacks, and there is a choice of four different salads. Main course dishes include venison timbale, piccata of pork fillet and beef and mushroom pie among a choice of ten. There are also pasta selections, vegetarian choices and a selection of ploughman's, sandwiches, sweets and hot drinks. Dating from 1680, the building was originally three cottages and a stable, and always included an alehouse. Beams, inglenook fireplaces and flagstone floors in some bar areas attest its age. Brassware and a large collection of chamberpots decorate the pub interior, while window-boxes of flowers add a touch of rural charm outside. The telephone number is 01590 673177.

The Red Lion, Boldre

uncertainty as to its origin, but suggests it may be an old name for the Lymington River, on which Boldre lies. This seems likely. Indeed, our old friend D. H. Moutray Read, in his *Highways and Byways in Hampshire*, published in 1908, unequivocally gives Boldre as an alternative name for the river. Support for this conclusion may be gleaned from the fact that the Lymington River, or Highland Water as it is known in its upper reaches, has its source not far from an area called Bolderwood, in the heart of the New Forest, well west of Lyndhurst. Another authority has suggested that the name 'Boldre' derives from a Celtic term meaning 'full stream', which adds further weight to this theory.

Where Boldre ends and Pilley begins would be hard for a stranger to discern without the help of a wayside notice. The name of Boldre's neighbour perhaps derives from the Old English 'pil-leah', meaning 'a wood or clearing where stakes are obtained', or so Mills informs us, not in connection with Pilley in Hampshire but with a northern England namesake.

Walhampton, one might guess, means something like 'home farm by the spring', the Old English for spring (or well) being 'waella'. Walhampton House, now a school, was originally the home of the Burrard family, one of whose more notable members was Admiral Sir Harry Burrard Neale. It was in memory of Sir Harry, who put down the mutiny at the Nore and was MP for Lymington way back in the days of rotten boroughs, that the Walhampton Monument was raised following his death in 1840. Sir Harry was a friend of William IV, the 'Sailor King', whose widow, Queen Adelaide, was one of several royals who associated themselves with the erection of the monument, a lofty pillar looming beside a lane followed on this walk. It dominates the view as one looks east from Lymington, which various Burrards served as mayors, in Parliament, or in other ways for over 400 years.

Walk 6

Distance: *Allow 3 hours for this five-and-a-quarter mile walk.*

Immediately east of The Red Lion turn right from the road called Rope Walk to follow Boldre Lane south between trees and houses for nearly half a mile. You then turn left just before the entrance to Shallowmead Nurseries to follow a narrow, sunken, tree-shaded metalled lane. This is signposted as leading to a ford 'unsuitable for motors'. In fact the metalled lane becomes a mere footpath a few yards short of the Lymington River, which you cross by means of an iron-railed footbridge directly alongside the ford.

Where tarmac resumes on the far side of the winding, full-bodied river, carry on ahead for a few yards before turning right through a gate to follow a signposted bridleway, which may be somewhat muddy after periods of wet weather, especially if cattle which graze the adjacent riverside marsh have been leaving their hoofmarks on it. You now head south with trees to your left and the reed-bordered river, with more trees beyond it, to your right. When farm buildings followed by cottages materialise to your left, turn left through a wooden gate to follow an uphill path between two dwellings. This path leads into a concrete road which you follow ahead, uphill, with trees on your right screening Vicars Hill, where William Gilpin lived.

Towle's Restaurant, Walhampton.
Although not a pub as such, this licensed restaurant en route, with its well-appointed bar and internal patio area, makes an ideal halfway house where you can relax over a pint of Royal Oak or Ringwood Bitter or one of three draught lagers while toying with the bar menu. This is likely to offer items such as half a chicken with vegetables, deep fried scampi or steak and chips, chargrilled sirloin steak and chips, and poached trout with side salad, not to mention smoked salmon with brown bread and a range of other salads as well as ploughman's and various sweets. During the week there is also a full lunchtime and evening a la carte menu. Food orders are taken between 1200-1430 and 1900-2130. A functions room seating up to 80 people has recently been added to the facilities at this extremely popular venue, the telephone number of which is 01590 673113.

Fleur-de-Lys Inn, Pilley.
With its whitewashed front and eyebrow windows peeping out from under the thatch, this is a picture of old world delight at the heart of a rural Forest community well away from the busier roads. Landlords dating back to AD1498 are listed in the Jacob Armitage bar, which, like the Beverley of Arnwood bar, is named after characters in Captain Marryat's 'Children of the New Forest.' The inn is mentioned in Conan Doyle's historical novel 'The White Company'. Alcoholic stimulants are said to have been sold here since 1096, only 30 years after the Battle of Hastings, so this may well be the oldest pub in the New Forest. A flagstoned entrance,

exposed beams and brickwork emphasise its vintage character, and hams used to be smoked in the chimney above an open fireplace. Brews available include Whitbread Best Bitter Morland's Old Speckled Hen and Marston's Pedigree. Thatcher's cider is also on draught. The bar menu lists items ranging from chicken liver pate, prawn open sandwiches, and crab claws with dips and salad garnish to sausage, haddock or breaded scampi with dips, ploughman's, curries, pastas, steaks, chicken dishes, breast of duck in honey and grapefruit sauce with fresh vegetables. Watch the board for daily specials, and there is a good choice of sweets. Lunchtime food may be ordered until 1400 on weekdays and until 1330 on Sundays while evening food orders are taken until 2130 on weekdays and 2100 on Sundays. Pub openings are 1100-1430 (until 1400 in winter) and 1800-2230 Mondays to Thursdays and until 2300 Fridays and Saturdays, Sunday openings hours being 1200-1430 and 1900-2230. Well-behaved children are welcome and there are swings for them in the garden. Walkers using the pub may use the pub car park. The telephone number is 01590 672158.

Emerging soon past the right-hand entrance to Southlands School, you join School Lane. About ten yards along this, with a large oak in the centre of a grassy triangle to your right, fork left to follow Hundred Lane. At the end of a walled garden on the right-hand side of this, turn right to follow a grass-and-gravelly track through woodland, soon joining a gravel road which you follow ahead through fenced farmland with views towards Lymington on your right.

This brings you out on to the Beaulieu-Lymington road opposite Walhampton House, the old Burrard family home and now a school. As you follow this road right-handed you pass Towle's Restaurant on your left before turning left to follow winding Monument Lane, one of those placid, tree-lined byways where motor traffic is still sparse enough for walking to be a pleasure. A tree-ringed hump on the right of this supports the Walhampton Monument, a tall stone pillar suggestive of Cleopatra's Needle. Inscriptions on four sides highlight events in the life of Admiral Sir Harry Burrard Neale, the man it was raised to commemorate, and, in the fashion of its period, wax lyrical to the point of excess about his qualities and achievements.

At this point you join The Solent Way, a long distance walking route from Milford-on-Sea to Emsworth which follows the coast wherever it can but is frequently forced to deviate inland and to follow roads instead of paths. The Solent Way leads you on along Monument Lane to where you can glimpse the yacht-studded estuary of the Lymington River, not far ahead and a little to your right.

At the corner of a gravelled approach on your left to a house called Halyards a Solent Way sign directs you along this to where a gap in the fence ahead of you where the driveway turns right to the house itself precedes a tall-hedged footpath. As you follow this it soon emerges from bordering trees to cross a farm track and continue ahead along the left-hand edge of a field. At the end of this you enter a wood to follow a well-defined path leading on ahead. After crossing a stile on your right, the path carries on in the same direction as hitherto, with a fence screening a house on your right and a wood now on your left. Beyond a foot-bridge over a stream a section of this path, which was once very muddy after rain, has been raised and gravelled to make it firm and dry as it rises through woodland before

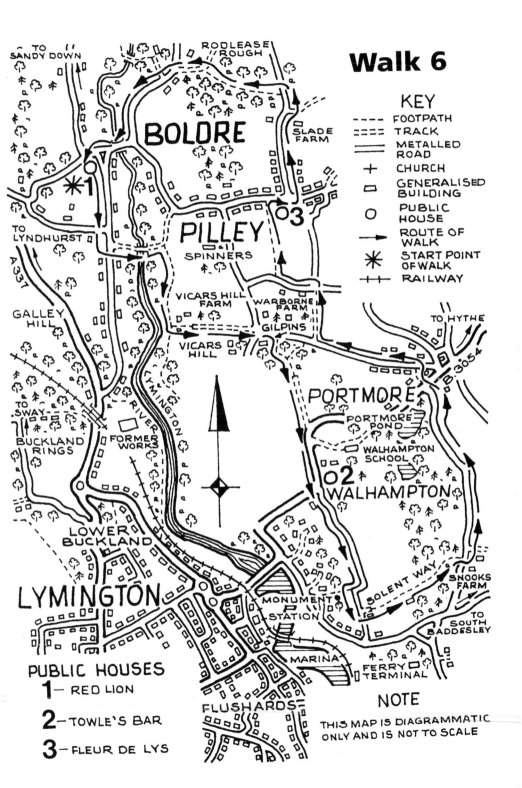

The Lymington River south of Boldre

emerging on to Snooks Lane, another quiet byway very much like Monument Lane and a pleasure to walk along.

As you follow Snooks Lane left-handed the Solent Way almost immediately turns right but you continue straight ahead. Portmore Pond can be glimpsed in private grounds to your left half a mile or so to the north a short distance before you emerge on to the Lymington-Beaulieu road. A very few yards along this to your right you follow a hedged grass path to your left, soon emerging on to another road at the western end of the hamlet of Portmore.

Follow this road left-handed for a few hundred yards into open countryside, then turn right by a footpath signpost to follow a track, hedged on the left and fenced on the right, to where a short footpath section from an adjacent farmyard entrance leads out on to a road which you follow left-handed. Where this road soon curves left, cross a stile by a footpath sign on your right to follow a path along the right-hand edge of a field. After crossing a further stile at the end of this path you reach Pilley.

Joining a road here, follow it right-handed to pass the old world Fleur-de-Lys Inn on your right. Not many yards beyond this you turn left to follow Church Lane. Beyond where bordering houses end this crosses a wooded dip, just past the bottom of which a signposted, well-used footpath leads you left-handed. Ignore a path which angles left from this and carry on west through a brackeny area just below a wooded slope where tunnelling badgers have their home. Bordering fences flank your approach to a gravel track which you follow left-handed to join a lane. Follow this left-handed in its turn to reach the Pilley-Boldre road, which you follow right-handed across the Lymington River and so back to Boldre, where The Red Lion is on your left about 200 yards ahead.

Coastal Countryside near Pennington at Lymington

WALK 7
Allow 3 hours
4½ or 4 miles
Walk begins page 43

Background to the Walk

Pennington was a mediaeval manor and its name is believed to mean 'farmstead paying a penny rent', which certainly does not hint at any great crop-producing potential of the land in this part of Hampshire! Agriculture today is not a major local activity and in centuries gone by the sea was a main source of local employment. From early times until the 19th century extraction of salt from evaporated sea water was carried on at up to 13 salterns on the neighbouring marshes. This only ceased when Cheshire's salt mines were developed as a cheaper source of this commodity. The method employed here was to let sea-water into shallow salt-pans, which would then be sealed off for evaporation to proceed. When this reached a certain point, the resultant brine would be boiled until all that was left was salt.

The Chequers Inn's lonely situation is linked with the saltworks once so close to it. Outgoing consignments of salt were checked here for tax purposes, hence apparently its name, the landlord told me. Working with salt sounds a thirsty business, and The Chequers Inn was well placed to restore body fluids to salt workers on their way home from the day's labours.

With the salterns consigned to history, Pennington Marshes is an important nature reserve to which vast numbers of water-loving birds flock every winter. Migrant species from the Arctic congregate not only on the freshwater marsh but also on the extensive mudflats exposed at low tide. This saltmarsh area has developed on accumulated silt protected against

Maps
Landranger 1:50,000
Sheet 196
1:25,000
Outdoor Leisure 22, New Forest
Map Reference of Start/Finish
SZ322936

How to get there
The Chequers Inn, at Lower Woodside, lies near the end of Ridgeway Lane, a quiet, hedged cul-de-sac forking left from the road that heads south from Pennington Cross, a roundabout on A337 half-a-mile on the Christchurch side of Lymington. From Southampton follow A3024 and A35 to Lyndhurst and A337 south from there via Brockenhurst to skirt Lymington, where A337 turns west for Pennington Cross. From Bournemouth head east along A35 to the eastern end of Christchurch bypass and then follow A337 via Highcliffe to skirt New Milton and bypass Everton village en route to Pennington Cross, where you turn right. Immediately on leaving the roundabout the lane signposted to Lower Pennington divides, the left-hand one being Ridgeway Lane. Disregard all side turnings from this until you reach The Chequers Inn on your right, just over half-a-mile ahead. Wilts & Dorset buses on services 56 and 56A from Southampton and Lyndhurst

and 112 from Hythe and Beaulieu connect at Lymington with local services 117 and 119 and with services 122 and 123 to and from Bournemouth, which pass through Pennington.

Pub facilities
Chequers Inn, Lower Woodside
Part of the charm of this pub is its quiet situation along a pleasant rural byway on the seaward side of Pennington, though with the sea still half-a-mile distant. Built about 1670, it has a creeper-covered front and a homely interior. Summer afternoon barbecues are held on the patio, and there is a garden at the back. Brews include Wadworth 6X and draught Bass as well as two guest ales drawn in the traditional way from hand-pumps. The pub is noted for fish dishes, such as grilled lemon sole and monkfish with tomato and garlic. A typical menu also offers soup, pate or salad starters, Italian pasta, vegetable risotto, roast rack of lamb with a coarse-grained mustard sauce, sirloin and rump steaks and mixed grills. Bar snacks include lasagne, chilli, burgers, fish and chips and scampi. There are facilities for children. Pub-using walkers may use the pub car park and there is additional space to park in the road outside. Opening hours are 1100-1430ish and 1800-2300 on weekdays and all day from 1200-2230 on Sundays, although this may vary depending upon prevailing conditions. Food may be ordered between 1200-1400 and 1900-2200 (2130 Sundays). Telephone number is 01590 673415.

The Chequers Inn, Lower Woodside

wave action from the open English Channel by the long shingle spit at the Solent's western end. The spit forms a pebbly promontory at the end of which looms Hurst Castle, built by Henry VIII as part of his south coast defences against the French and garrisoned until quite recently.

At the landward end of the shingle spit, between it and the outflow of the Avon Water rivulet, is Keyhaven, a yachtsman's paradise. Twelfth century Kihavene was apparently 'a haven where cows were shipped'. Seven centuries later it was the haunt of a certain Colonel Peter Hawker, whose claim to fame was his adeptness at slaughtering wildfowl on Keyhaven's mudflats. The cottage where he lived is still pointed out. Just in case you might miss it, it bears the name-plaque 'Hawker's Cottage', while the pub next door is called The Gun as a further reminder of Hawker's method of exploiting the local wildlife.

The sea wall protecting Keyhaven and Pennington Marshes from inundation by high tides was undergoing extensive repairs when we first tried this walk. Part of the public footpath along it was temporarily closed in consequence, making it necessary for us to use a diversionary path which is probably worth trying as an alternative route anyway, so a description of it is included here. We went back later to try out the coastal route when the work had been completed and the path, a very popular one, was open for use again.

Walk 7

Distance: *Allow 3 hours for this walk of either four-and-a-half or four miles.*

Having left The Chequers Inn behind you on your right, within yards fork right from Lower Woodside, a southerly extension of Ridgeway Lane, with Chequers Green on your left, to follow a private road which is also the beginning of a public footpath. A few yards along this, at the approach to the private entrance to Pennington House, turn right towards a field entry-point, then almost immediately cross a stile on your left. Follow a fenced path to a stile beyond which you follow the right-hand edge of a meadow for a few yards before crossing another stile, in the hedgerow on your right, to follow the left-hand edge of the arable field you now enter. This brings you to yet another stile, after crossing which you continue along the left-hand edge of the next field to a sixth stile preceding Lower Pennington Lane.

Follow this left-handed, past farm buildings, as far as a right-hand metal gate adjoined by a footpath sign. You now follow a path around the gate and along the metalled lane you now enter to a further gate where roadmetal ends. Walk round the gate to follow the grass-and-gravel track that leads ahead here skirting left of a fairly substantial lake on a former gravel extraction site. Here in winter we saw large numbers of handsome tufted duck, squadrons of coots with their distinctive snowy-white foreheads and, almost inevitably, gulls. Just beyond this man-made nature sanctuary is a metalled lane which you cross. Go over a stile adjoining a gate directly opposite and fork left at a junction of tracks here to follow the one signposted as a footpath. Extensive gravel workings flank the grass-and-gravel track you now follow ahead, in a fairly straight line, across flat ground for some distance. All this land will eventually be restored to agricultural use, or so the powers-that-be assure us.

The Gun, Keyhaven
Should you decide to start your walk at this Keyhaven pub instead of at The Chequers you can use the public car park opposite. The pub occupies a 17th century building which in earlier times was a chapel and also a mortuary. Today, despite this history, it is a lively watering-hole for the yachting fraternity, noted for maritime bric-a-brac as well as a large collection of old matchboxes and cigarette cards. Panelled walls enhance the period atmosphere and it has a large garden, a children's room and a patio at the side. Opening hours are 1100-1500 and 1800-2300 on weekdays and 1200-1500 and 1900-2230 on Sundays. A choice of six real ales includes Ringwood Forty-Niner, Marston's Pedigree, Morland's Old Speckled Hen, Fuller's London Pride and Flower's Original, with one or two of these sometimes being substituted by guest ales and with Murphy's Irish stout also on tap. Home-made wines are another speciality. Food ordering times are 1200-1415 and 1800-2115 (from 1900 on Sundays) with a choice of such starters, main courses and snacks as soup, prawn cocktail, plaice, lemon sole, quarter roast chicken, seafood crepes, breaded squid strips, garlic mushrooms, battered cod fillets, gammon and pineapple, poached salmon, crab when in season, jumbo sausage, various salad platters, garlic battered chicken, goujons, ploughman's, jacket potatoes and assorted sandwiches. There is also a good selection of sweets. The telephone number is 01590 642391.

Quarrying scars give way to thickets of gorse and plantations of young conifers and broadleaved trees as the track you follow heads south, being flanked at one point by Keyhaven-Lymington Nature Reserve with its marshland greenery. Disregard a diverted footpath which branches left and carry on to where a metal gate with a stile alongside it precedes your emergence on to another unmetalled track. As you follow the latter right-handed you soon reach another metal gate, which you walk round to continue along what is now a public road open to ordinary traffic.

Only a little way ahead now is a bridge across the outflow of the Avon Water rivulet. Directly beyond this is Keyhaven, where Hawker's Cottage confronts you to the right of The Gun Inn. At the height of summer this otherwise placid, end-of-the-road backwater is a hive of yachting activity. The winding inlet which leads to the open water of the Solent is also traversed by a ferry shuttling to and from Hurst Castle, clearly visible from Keyhaven at the end of a long bank of shingle probing towards the Isle of Wight.

Having sampled what The Gun Inn has to offer, return across Avon Water, directly beyond which the sea wall path to Lymington turns right. Not far along this, on our winter walk, we paused for picnic sandwiches and to watch the first of many migrant brent geese from the Arctic flying to and from their low tide feeding grounds along this shore.

After skirting the yacht-filled channel between Keyhaven and the Solent, the sea wall path steers its way around Keyhaven Marshes on the landward side, where gorsy expanses and rough pastureland contrast with the bird-thronged mudlands exposed by the ebb tide to your right. We found one section of the sea wall badly eroded, making it necessary to walk along the adjacent shingly strand where the footpath proper had crumbled away, a state of affairs which had not altered when the author walked all these routes afresh to check them out for this new edition. The wall and its surmounting path very soon re-assert themselves and do not part company again. From this point onwards the wall has been strengthened in the fairly recent past to provide a very substantial bastion against encroachment by salt water on to the fresh-water marsh inland.

Bring binoculars and a bird-recognition guide to make the most of opportunities to identify a host of species which make this wet world their home. Low tide brings wading birds in their multitudes to probe for food in the tidal ooze. Watch out at all times for oystercatchers, redshank, curlew, herons and, on the creeks and marshland pools, smart-plumaged shelduck, one of our largest wild duck species. If you walk this way in autumn or winter many other seasonal visitors, ranging from dunlin to black-tailed godwits, red-breasted merganser, eider duck and large flocks of brent geese from the Arctic, as already mentioned, may be expected. Birds we saw when we walked here in winter ranged from sparrow-sized rock pipits to a solitary short-eared owl hunting the freshwater marsh in daylight — this last was a pleasing sight indeed of a species scarce in southern England. On another occasion I was lucky enough to see that

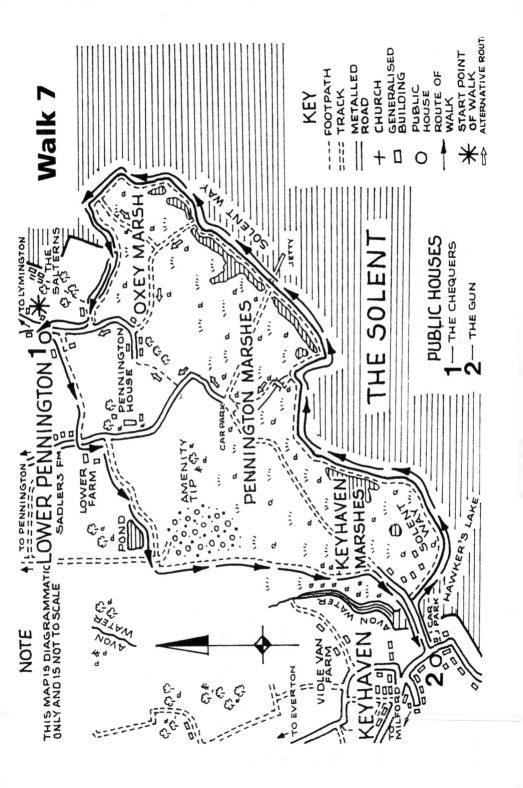

Walk 7

NOTE
THIS MAP IS DIAGRAMMATIC ONLY AND IS NOT TO SCALE

KEY
---- FOOTPATH
==== TRACK
—— METALLED ROAD
+ CHURCH
☐ GENERALISED BUILDING
○ PUBLIC HOUSE
↑ ROUTE OF WALK
✳ START POINT OF WALK
⇨ ALTERNATIVE ROUTE

PUBLIC HOUSES
1 — THE CHEQUERS
2 — THE GUN

THE SOLENT

OXEY MARSH

PENNINGTON MARSHES

KEYHAVEN MARSHES

SOLENT WAY

JETTY

CAR PARK

AMENITY TIP

POND

LOWER FARM

SADLERS FM

PENNINGTON HOUSE

LOWER PENNINGTON

THE SALTERNS

TO LYMINGTON

TO PENNINGTON

AVON WATER

VIDLE VAN FARM

KEYHAVEN

TO MILFORD

TO EVERTON

HAWKER'S LAKE

SOLENT SWAY

CAR PARK

The Gun Inn, Keyhaven

snowy-plumaged miniature heron, the little egret, a once rare visitor which has been turning up more often in recent years.

Another particular pleasure of a walk along this wall between Pennington Marshes and salt water is the marked contrast between the level terrain and seascape close at hand and the looming contours of the land across the water, some three miles distant. The Isle of Wight, where woods and downlands rear beyond the Solent seaway, has an intimacy here with the mainland which results from its being closer than at any other point, presenting a picture of exceptionally quiet, come-hither enchantment.

Within two miles the sea wall path bends left alongside an inlet. Across the upper reaches of this a path branches right over a sluice-gate but you keep straight on, descending some steps and soon turning right over a stile. Your path continues past the head of the creek to emerge on to an oak-bordered lane. Follow this right-handed to arrive back at The Chequers Inn, about 200 yards along it.

The shorter route back follows a track which turns left, as already mentioned, where the sea wall bends sharply right about a mile after leaving Keyhaven. The track leads a fairly straight course across Pennington Marshes, converging with another track as it emerges on to a metalled lane, which you follow to the right. Not many yards beyond where this lane takes a right-angled bend to the left a fenced gravel path leads you right-handed, skirting right of a tree-surrounded pond favoured by swans before maturing into a narrow metalled lane which serves some cottages. This delightful byway gently winds its way back to The Chequers Inn, not many hundred yards ahead.

Another pleasant conclusion is to continue along the sea wall path for a further half-mile or so before turning left to follow not the first but the second, third or fourth gated track heading across the adjacent marshes. These tracks unite to bring you out on to the byway last referred to which you follow right-handed for a very short distance to The Chequers Inn.

Streamside and Shore near Milford-on-Sea

WALK 8
Up to 4 hours
6 miles
Walk begins page 49

Background to the Walk

Hampshire's Downton is a very small place on the notoriously twisty stretch of A337 that runs between Everton and New Milton, bypassing Milford-on-Sea and the coast. You could almost be forgiven for passing through it in a hurry and hardly noticing that it exists. Lacking a church, it has for its focal point the Royal Oak pub, right on the crossroads at its centre. The pub has been there for 300 years and the oak which shades part of its front may well be as old, though not perhaps royal. The name Downton, experts tell us, means 'farmstead on or by the hill or down' and indeed farmland still surrounds Downton. Of hill or down there is no sign, although it has to be borne in mind that the term 'down', as used in Hampshire, is not exclusive to the county's chalk hill areas — as witness Emery Down, near Lyndhurst, and Browndown, near Gosport.

Delving into the past, we find that 13th century Downton was recorded as 'Duneketon'. This became 'Donketon' the following century, which firmed up as 'Donckton' between the 16th and 18th centuries, then to become 'Dounckton' or, as some would have it, 'Dunkerton'. Whatever the origin of 'our' Downton, it appears to have first come to notice during the reign of Henry III as the property of the heirs of one Elizabeth de Granges, who held it as lessees, in effect, of the lord of the manor of Christchurch.

Between Downton and the coast, just a mile away to the south-west, is a tract of unspoilt countryside the survival of which, in these parts, must be counted almost as a miracle. This makes the initial approach to

Maps
Landranger 1:50,000
Sheets 195 and 196
1:25,000
Outdoor Leisure 22, New Forest
Map Reference of Start/Finish
SZ269934

How to get there
Not to be confused with Downton in Wiltshire's Avon Valley, the Downton where this walk starts is in Hampshire on A337, the Christchurch-Lymington road, 2 miles east of New Milton. From Southampton follow A3024 and A35 to Lyndhurst and A337 from there via Brockenhurst, Lymington and Pennington. Alternatively, follow A3024 and A35 to the western end of Totton's southern bypass, A326 from there to Dibden Purlieu, A3054 from there via Beaulieu to Lymington and from there follow A337 via Pennington to Downton. From Bournemouth follow A35 to the eastern end of Christchurch bypass and from there follow A337 via Highcliffe and the outskirts of New Milton. Bus access from Southampton is via Wilts & Dorset services 56 or 56A to Lymington and service 123 or 124 from there to Milford-on-Sea, starting there instead of at Downton. Milford-on-Sea can be reached from Bournemouth by Wilts & Dorset bus services 123 and 124. There is no

service to Downton itself.

Pub facilities
Royal Oak, Downton
Erected in 1713, this quiet
country pub was run by the
same family for well over a
century until quite recently,
and its present management
carries on the same tradition of
providing good, home-cooked
food and other refreshment in a
friendly, welcoming
atmosphere. Opening hours on
weekdays are 1130-1500 and
1800-2300, Sunday opening
being from 1200-1500 and
1900-2230. Brews on draught
include Whitbread Best Bitter,
Ringwood Best Bitter, Flower's
Original and Fuller's London
Pride as well as Guinness,
Murphy's Irish stout and Stella
and Heineken lagers. Inch's
Strongbow cider is also
available on draught. Food
orders are taken from 1130
(1200 on Sundays) until 1400
and from 1800-2130 (1900-
2115 on Sundays). Menu items
have been greatly extended to
include around 50 dishes,
among which is a very wide
choice of blackboard specials
which are changed at regular
intervals. Those who want
nothing more than a snack to
sustain them while they are
walking might opt for a brown
or white bread sandwich
containing, for example, sliced
honey roast ham, grated mature
Cheddar cheese, egg
mayonnaise, tuna, cucumber
and mayonnaise, or chicken.
There are also five types of
toasted sandwiches and
Hampshire ploughman's
lunches with as many different
fillings as well as large jacket
potatoes served with butter and
a side salad and with a choice of
six different fillings. If a full-
blown meal is your preference,
starters range from prawn
cocktail, duck liver pate and
garlic mushrooms to soup of the

The Royal Oak, Downton

the gravelly cliff overlooking Christchurch Bay a very
pleasant cross-country walk with an equally pleasing
culmination: a stretch of shoreline viewed from a
footpath high enough above sea-level to present a
panorama extending from Dorset in the west to the
Isle of Wight in the south-east.

Modern Milford is very different. Delightful
enough is the triangular village green, but among its
flanking shops and cottages there are not many which
pre-date development of the one-time sleepy village
into a coastal retirement haven. This was instigated in
1887 by landowner Colonel William Cornwallis-West,
its more outstanding elements being a string of
seaside dwellings of a size and type appropriate to
the time when they were built. Before this happened,
Milford-on-Sea was just Milford. The mill must have
been on Danes Stream, a substantial brook whose
bosky meanderings gladden the homeward stretch of
this walk for those who set out from Downton, or its
outset stage for walkers starting at Milford. This
stream reaches the sea via Sturt pond, a brackish lake
which fills with salt water when incoming tides from
the Solent reverse the flow of the brook's seaward
section.

Jutting out for a mile between the Solent and the
open Channel is Hurst Beach, a shingle spit created
by tidal action over the ages and nowadays reinforced

artificially to keep it in being as a barrier against rough seas flooding in to erode low-lying land on its sheltered side. At the end of the spit, and nearer the Isle of Wight than the Hampshire mainland, is Henry VIII's Hurst Castle, important for coastal defence until well within living memory. Nowadays maintained as an ancient monument, it is accessible either on foot along the length of the shingle spit or, in the summer season, by ferry from Keyhaven, just east of Milford.

Walk 8

Distance: *Allow 4 hours for this six mile walk.*

Follow for a few hundred yards the twisty, tree-bordered lane which heads south from Downton crossroads. Watch out for a right-hand metal gate flanked by a double-stepped wooden stile, which you cross. The grass-centred gravel lane you now follow is fenced on your left and hedged at first on your right, with fields on both sides. Where the right-hand hedge and fence soon end, continue ahead along a field-edge path to the near side of a wooded gully. Here you turn left to cross a metal-barred, stepless stile and follow a fenced path south, with the wood to your right. Summertime herbage is apt to encroach here, but we were pleased to find it had been trimmed back for walkers.

At the wood end cross a second metal stile, where a waymarking arrow keeps you on course as you keep straight on at first, with a fence and field to your left and scattered trees in a valley pasture to your right. Your path soon veers right-handed to cross the grassy valley, where a concrete bridge preceded and followed by stepless double-barred stiles takes you across Danes Stream. Follow the left-hand meadow-edge fence uphill to a double metal-barred stile where a footpath sign directs you slightly right-handed.

Here you reach the Milford-New Milton road, a few yards along which, on its far side as you head right, is Taddiford car park. A double-fenced gravel path leads from this between pastures to the clifftop, on our way towards which a migrant wheatear flashed

day and mousse salad. You can choose from six different salad dishes or from nine main course items such as steak and ale pie, grilled gammon steak, cottage pie, lasagne al forno, sweet and sour pork and Malaysian chicken curry. A good choice of seafood and vegetarian dishes as well as a varied children's menu and a good range of desserts may also tempt you. Children are welcome in the bar. There is a rear garden and a covered patio area with wrought iron furniture. Walkers wishing to leave their cars in the pub car park risk being wheel-clamped if they do so without first asking permission. Alternative parking space is available in a lay-by alongside the main road a few yards west of the pub. The telephone number is 01590 642297.

Smugglers Inn, Milford-on-Sea

Open all day on weekdays from 1000-2300 and from 1200-2230 on Sundays, this village pub with its low-beamed ceilings dates from 1803 and was originally The Crown. Public car parks are adjacent. As well as Flower's Original and Boddington's, which are regularly available, two or three guest real ales are always on tap and are changed frequently. Also on draught are Guinness and Murphy's Irish stout as well as Heineken, Heineken Export and Stella lagers and Strongbow and Scrumpy Jack cider. There is also a large selection of bottled beers. Food ordering times are 1100-1430 and 1800-2100 from Mondays to Fridays and all day from 1100-2100 on Saturdays and Sundays. The food menu lists a good choice of starters and main courses, daily specials including a roast of the day and a daily three course lunch as well as basket meals, salads, ploughman's and vegetarian dishes. Specials include strips of beef in fresh ginger and soya sauce, chicken Provencale, steak and kidney pie, seafood crepes, home-made chilli, curry, sweet and sour pork and lasagne with salad. A good choice of sweets is available. There is live music on Friday and Saturday evenings and in the large garden there are swings, slides and a children's 'smugglers boat'. The telephone number is 01590 644414.

its brilliant white rump as it flew out from one of the fence-posts. This was towards the end of summer, a time of year when birds of this species are preparing to depart to warmer latitudes for the winter and bracing themselves for a cross-Channel flight as the first stage of their southerly journey.

On the day of our walk the clifftop overlooked a placid bay where the rhythmic swish of waves against shingle was the only sound apparent. We made our way down the broken cliff-face to sit on a concrete slab close to the tideline and watch the terns, those so-called sea-swallows which look superficially like gulls but are so much more graceful.

These cliffs of gravel and clay are badly subject to erosion — not so much from the sea itself, which has the pebble beach against which to vent most of its wrath, but from wind and rain beating against them as tempests sweep in from the Channel.

Regaining the clifftop, if you have enjoyed a brief break on the water's edge, follow the coast path eastwards, with fields to your left and the cliff to your right. Part-gravel and part-clay surfaced, the path becomes tarred and gravelled as you head east past Hordle Cliff, a popular bathing spot where the beach may be reached by steps from a public car park. Wayside seats become a feature as road and clifftop almost converge at the western end of Milford-on-Sea. The tar-and-gravel path ends where you reach and skirt a complex of derelict concrete buildings to continue along a flagstoned path, with beach huts now to your right, the cliff having ended.

The path becomes shingly as you approach and pass Marine Cafe, with its car park, beyond which a shingle bank to your right at the beginning of Hurst Spit flanks your approach to a robust footbridge where you cross Danes Stream at its outflow from Sturt Pond. As already noted, rising tides convert this to an inflow, flooding Sturt Pond with salt water.

With your back to the sea, you now head left along a path of gravel and flint, with Sturt Pond to your left and a caravan park to your right. Streamside reeds and maritime pines precede the point where a stepped path joins a metalled cul-de-sac which you follow left-ahead, with dwellings to your right. Within a very short distance you once again follow a brookside path from a point where The Solent Way's blue arrow logo identifies the route as part of the long distance coastal walk of this name from Milford-on-Sea to Emsworth.

Another stout footbridge soon takes you back over the fish-haunted Danes Stream to emerge by way of a car park, adjoining which are public conveniences. This brings you out on to a road which you follow right-handed to cross Danes Stream again. You then skirt right of Milford's The Smugglers to your right as you approach the main village road, which you cross straight over

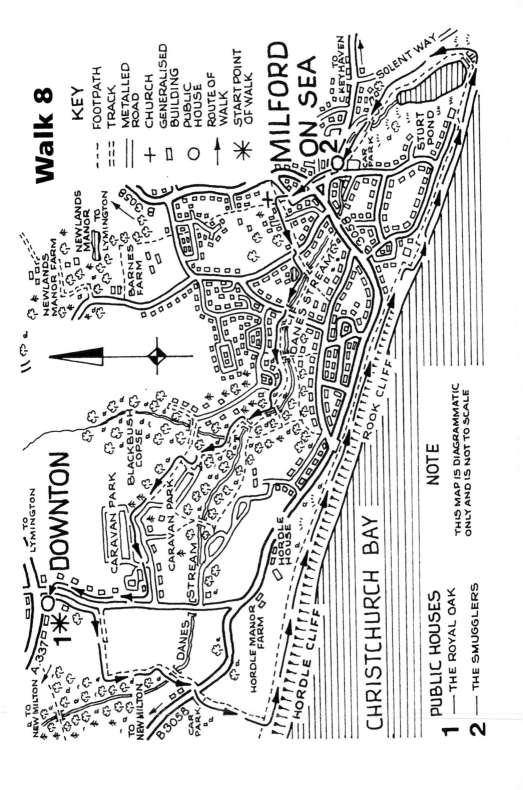

Walk 8

KEY

– – –	FOOTPATH
═ ═	TRACK
———	METALLED ROAD
+	CHURCH
▢	GENERALISED BUILDING
○	PUBLIC HOUSE
↑	ROUTE OF WALK
✳	START POINT OF WALK

MILFORD ON SEA

2

CAR PARK

STURT POND

TO KEYHAVEN

Solent Way

TO LYMINGTON

B3058

NEWLANDS MANOR FARM

NEWLANDS MANOR FARM

NEWLANDS MANOR

BARNES FARM

DOANES STREAM

ROOK CLIFF

DOWNTON

TO LYMINGTON

1

D
TO NEW MILTON A.337

B3058

TO NEW MILTON

CARAVAN PARK

BLACKBUSH COPSE

CARAVAN PARK

CARAVAN PARK

STREAM

DANES

HORDLE HOUSE

HORDLE MANOR FARM

CAR PARK

HORDLE CLIFF

CHRISTCHURCH BAY

NOTE

THIS MAP IS DIAGRAMMATIC ONLY AND IS NOT TO SCALE

PUBLIC HOUSES

1 —— THE ROYAL OAK

2 —— THE SMUGGLERS

to follow a road called Church Hill.

The church is at the top of this incline, where there has been a place of worship for perhaps 1,000 years. Spare time to look around All Saints: spacious and dignified is how the church was summed up in that monumental work of reference, the *Victoria County History of Hampshire*, published before the First World War, and it is certainly both of these things despite its modest size.

With the church to your right after you have left it, follow a churchyard path as far as a lamp-post and there turn left to leave the churchyard by way of a metal kissing-gate. This precedes a hedge-bowered sunken footway very suitably called Love Lane, which leads to a metalled road called The Orchard. Cross this and follow the path which continues ahead to the next road, which you follow right-handed past the first house. You then turn left to follow a hedged path to a concrete bridge over a stream, beyond which a pond overlooked by houses lies to your right.

Directly ahead is our old friend the Danes Stream, winding its way through a woody valley whose course you follow for some distance after crossing a metal footbridge and then turning right at a footpath T-junction. Sycamores shade your gravelled footway, with Danes Stream between you and houses to your right. Cross the next road and then bridge the stream once more. Ignore a right-turning path and keep right-ahead at the next path junction, disregarding a path which diverges left to bridge the stream in its own turn.

At the next T-junction of paths turn left to bridge the stream, after crossing which your path bends right to follow the valley. Disregard the next right-turning path, which bridges the brook almost immediately, but take the next one, which crosses Danes Stream and a subsequent tributary brook before becoming fenced and soon climbing right-handed to enter a holiday caravan park. If route directions from Love Lane up to here seem slightly confusing, the important thing to remember is to disregard all paths that lead away from the stream valley until you have no option but to enter the caravan park. Here you take the first service road to the right to climb to the upper edge of the site by way of a path leading on ahead from the service road to a T-junction of paths, from which a fenced and hedged path leads you left-handed.

This path soon joins a metalled road emerging from the caravan park, which you follow right-ahead. At first confined to ground to your left, the caravan park soon spills over to your right, where you presently pass the clubhouse of what announces itself as Shorefield Country Park. The name 'Shorefield' apparently dates from the 16th century, and was not dreamed up, as might be supposed, to suggest to prospective holiday visitors that the caravan park is nearer to the sea than it really is. Disregard all side-turnings and continue ahead until you emerge on to a winding country lane. Here you turn right for the final half-mile of your walk back to The Royal Oak at Downton.

Footpaths and Forest Tracks near Tiptoe

WALK 9
Up to 4 hours
7½ miles
Walk begins page 54

Background to the Walk

The New Forest's southern borderland is peppered with villages and hamlets which have grown in size and have sometimes coalesced as population has increased during the course of the 20th century. Tiptoe, between Sway and New Milton, is fairly typical of these places. Now quite a populous community, it began life as an insignificant appendage of the substantial parish of Hordle, stretching from the Forest itself to the coast beyond Milford-on-Sea. Although now somewhat over-shadowed by some of its faster-growing neighbours, Hordle in the past was a place whose importance matched its size. The Domesday Survey recorded it in AD1086 as 'Herdel'. Two centuries later this become 'Hordhill', which is closer to the name's original meaning, supposedly signifying a hill where treasure had been found.

Wootton, a mile west of Tiptoe, is not so much a village or even a hamlet as a scattering of dwellings which have sprung up at various times along the edge of the Forest proper. The placename Wootton is a common one meaning 'farmstead in or near a wood', which is as appropriate for this area today as it ever was. While nearby New Milton has grown from virtually nothing into a town in the course of a century, Wootton, just north of it, remains unsophisticatedly rustic, a home for people who love the countryside and especially for those who enjoy spending leisure time with horses.

The local farmland, if it may strictly be so described now, is given over almost entirely to providing

Maps
Landranger 1:50,000
Sheet 195
1:25,000
Outdoor Leisure 22, New Forest
Map Reference of Start/Finish
SZ257971

How to get there
From Southampton follow A3024 and then A35 west along Totton's southern bypass, then via Ashurst, around Lyndhurst and across the New Forest to Holmsley, at the far end of which turn left to follow B3058 for about 3 miles to where it crosses B3055 a mile north of New Milton. Now follow B3055 left for a mile to reach The Plough Inn on your left. From Bournemouth follow Wessex Way and A35 east around Christchurch and then north-east to a point half-a-mile beyond The Cat & Fiddle Inn at Hinton Admiral. Here turn right to follow B3055 for 3 miles to reach The Plough Inn on your left. Frequent trains between Southampton and Bournemouth stop at New Milton, from which Wilts & Dorset buses on services 121 and 122 between Bournemouth and Lymington pass through Hordle. A walk of about a mile from Hordle along Vaggs Lane will bring you to Tiptoe, where you turn left along B3055 to reach the Plough Inn on your right within about 200 yards.

Pub facilities
Plough Inn, Tiptoe
Open all day from 1100-2300 (1200-2230 on Sundays), this Whitbread Wayside Inn serves food from 1200-1400 and 1900-2200. Dating from 1630 and thought originally to have been a farmhouse, the pub has cob walls and interior panelling which go far to preserve its period atmosphere, while hanging baskets by the front entrance underline its country character. Families are well catered for, with no restriction on children except in the bar area. The garden includes a children's play area with slides and amusements. Two open fires enhance comfort in cold weather. Real ales are Flower's Original and Wadworth 6X. Whitbread Best Bitter, Boddington's Gold, Murphy's Irish stout, Guinness, Heineken and Stella lagers and Strongbow cider are also on draught. Home-cooked food highlights country pies among a good choice of bar snacks including four different ploughman's. The menu lists eight starters, four salad platters, ten main courses and five desserts, and there is a good selection of wines. Dogs are no problem, and pub-using walkers may leave their cars in the car park. The telephone number is 01425 610185.

The Rising Sun, Wootton
Although the present building dates from Victorian times there has been an inn on this Forest-edge site for centuries, we are told, and at one time this was probably a meeting point for smugglers handling illicit cargoes of spirits landed at night on the nearby coast. To meet the needs of our own time the pub, a Whitbread house, has recently undergone extensive refurbishment and enlargement of its facilities. Catering for all

The Plough Inn, Tiptoe

pasturage for horses. Pony paddocks keep you company as you follow the paths and byways of the earlier and later parts of this walk. On the route's middle section, within the Forest, many of the folk you will meet are likely to be local riders, exercising steeds whose home pastures are in the Tiptoe or Wootton areas.

The equestrian link is reinforced by repeated sightings of forest ponies, not only on the open heathland but in the timber inclosures theoretically fenced against these animals. Time was when New Forest commoners' animals and plantations of growing trees were kept fairly rigidly apart, for the good of the trees. Some of those entitled to exercise common rights, however, were not above being tempted to open a gate and allow their stock to enter the woods with all the lush grazing to be enjoyed there. Today they hardly need to bother — the ponies find their way in anyway, and once inside they tend to remain. Some years ago a chief forester, now retired, told me he reckoned there were more ponies in the 'forbidden' inclosures than out of them.

Walk 9

Distance: *Allow 4 hours for this seven-and-a-half mile walk.*
From The Plough Inn, at the westernmost extremity

of Tiptoe, head west for about one-third of a mile along B3055, a busy road with discontinuous grass verges along which you need to walk with care. After crossing the wooded valley of the Danes Stream, a substantial brook which winds south-east to meet salt water near Milford-on-Sea, you climb beyond to reach Danestream Farm Shop on your right. This has a forecourt where it just might be possible to obtain permission to park and thus cut out the preceding road walk — at any rate, there is no harm in asking!

Immediately beyond the farm shop turn right to follow a narrow metalled byway flanked by farm buildings on your right. Where this byway soon also divides into two parallel driveways separated by a hedge, follow the gravelled left-hand drive, which soon also divides. Here you bear right to follow a fenced grass path preceded and followed by farm gateways. Beyond the gate at the end of this your path continues ahead downhill along the left-hand edge of a meadow with woodland to your left. This brings you to a stile preceding a wooden footbridge over the Danes Stream. After crossing this brook your tree-shaded footpath rises between fences and then continues around the right-hand edge of a paddock to emerge by way of a stile on to a lane, which you follow right-handed. The lane immediately bends left to head north past scattered dwellings and horse paddocks. You next cross a metalled road to follow a gravel drive signposted as a public footpath. By the entrance to Broadley Farm, on your right, this driveway ends at the New Forest's edge, where a metal step on one of the bars of a locked gate ahead of you serves as a stile.

Cross this to reach the open forest, where you walk ahead for a few yards across grass to reach and follow right-handed a narrow but clearly-defined footpath. Where visible signs of a footpath end, continue ahead across grass towards gorse bushes straight ahead, then, by a telephone and power line post, turn right to join a Forest-edge gravel track which you follow left-handed. This fairly soon leads into a metalled road, which you follow ahead for a few yards before turning left where a 40mph speed restriction sign is painted on the road surface.

A gravelly path now leads you scenically downhill through scattered gorse clumps with the trees of Set Thorns Inclosure rising beyond the valley ahead. As

ages and tastes, it has become a very popular place of call for Forest visitors and their families. The comforts of the Victorian Bar, with its open fire for the colder months, are complemented by a rear pergola and tack room leading into a sizeable fenced garden. There is a pets corner with rabbits, goats and other animals appropriate to a New Forest setting, an aviary and a children's play area well-equipped to keep the younger generation safely amused. Opening times are 1100-2300 (1200-2230 on Sundays), and brews on draught include Ringwood Best Bitter, Flower's Original, Wadworth 6X, Boddington's, Murphy's Irish stout and Stella, Heineken and Heineken Export lagers. Thatcher's cider is also on draught. Food orders are taken all day from 1200-2200 seven days a week. Daily blackboard specials supplement a very extensive menu ranging from favourites such as steak and kidney pudding, lamb with chillies and coriander and braised beef au poivre to pies, savoury dishes, fish and chips, tasty bakes, quiches served hot, pastas, chargrills and roasts, and salads. There is a very good children's menu, and prices are sensible. As well as a large pub car park there is a corral where carriage drivers and riders can leave their vehicles and horses while taking a break at The Rising Sun! The telephone number is 01425 610360.

with so many Forest paths and tracks, this one divides and reunites and is joined by others at intervals, making it easy to take a wrong turning, but if you continue ahead until you reach the valley bottom and there bear half-right where another track joins your own from the left, you will keep on course for a wooden footbridge crossing the Avon Water rivulet. After heavy rain this may be preceded by a parallel shallow overflow which you will need Wellington boots to cross dry-footed, so be warned!

A few yards left of the footbridge is a ford used by horse-riders, and just ahead of you now is a gate where you enter Set Thorns Inclosure. The track that leads on into this wood becomes gravelled as it climbs between well-spaced oaks and pines intermixed with dense, dark conifers. Heading uphill, you take the second ride turning left through tallish pines and younger trees. This leads to a T-junction with another ride which bifurcates at this point, with its parallel courses reuniting as you follow it right-handed.

Where an oak-bordered clearing appears ahead fork left to join a gravel road which you follow to the left. A succession of oaks intermixed with hollies, dense young conifers, open areas, and a grove of tall hill-slope conifers rising impressively to your right flanks the woodland gravel road that now leads you towards where well-spaced oaks give shelter to a caravan camping site.

You now follow a track that bears left towards a gateway through which you leave Set Thorns Inclosure and head towards an arch underneath the old Brockenhurst-Ringwood railway. On the near side of this bear left again to follow a twisty track heading westward over gorse-and-brackeny heathland parallel with the former railway, with leftward views across the Avon Water valley towards wooded higher ground beyond. This brings you to an unfenced road which you follow to the left, keeping to parallel heathland tracks before bridging the Avon Water again.

Beyond this follow a gravel road right-handed through a gateway into Wootton Copse Inclosure. At a fork not far ahead you leave the gravel and bear left to follow a grass ride which soon joins another ride. It was while following this last ride right-ahead that we saw fallow deer as they burst out of riverside trees not far in front of us, raced up the ride for a few yards and then disappeared right-handed into thick cover once again.

We last saw them close to a ride-fork where you bear left to follow an uphill ride which joins a gravel track. Follow the latter left-handed through a gate and along the scenic southern margin of this inclosure in which oaks and pines provide a placid prospect to please the eye at every turn. This brings you back on to the road by which you crossed the Avon Water. From Broadley car park, on the road's far side a little way uphill, bear right to follow a heathland path uphill, parallel with the road, to The Rising Sun at Wootton, now directly ahead.

When you reach the pub turn right to head west in the Holmsley direction alongside the B3058. A little way along this, on your left, a public footpath sign precedes two stepless stiles which you cross to follow the right-hand edge of a

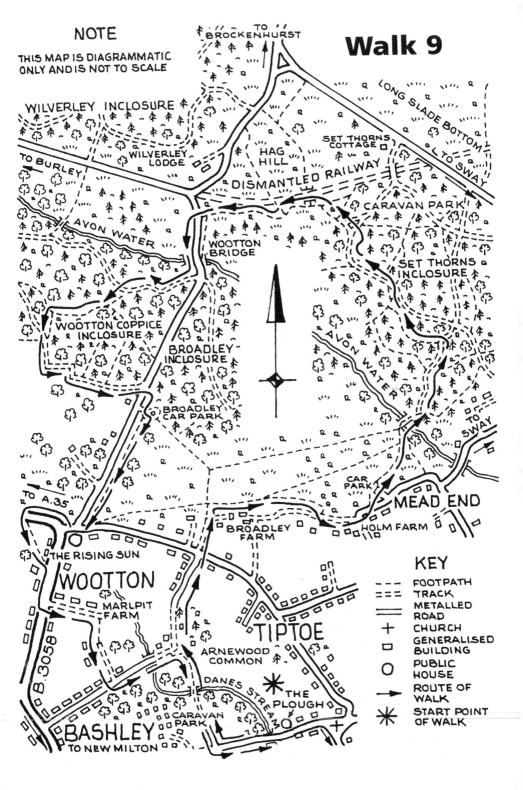

Forest scenery en route

paddock. At the end of this two further stepless stiles are followed by a fenced path with a ditch to your right. This leads to another stepless stile beyond which you continue across an area of rough grass with a wall to your right and a house on your left, to emerge over another stile on to a road, which you follow right-handed through the northern end of Bashley.

About 200 yards along this road, turn left by a postal pillar-box where a footpath sign points your way along tall-hedged Marlpits Lane. Follow this for a short distance to another footpath sign by a stile in a gap in the hedge to your right. Cross this stile and follow a fenced path between paddocks to a further stile preceding a gravel lane. This leads ahead to a T-junction with a metalled lane, which you follow left-handed past a right-hand wood and across a tree-lined dip where you bridge a very infant Danes Stream.

Your lane becomes briefly gravelled before bringing you to the point where it takes a right-angled turn to the left and where you turn right by a footpath sign you will recognise from the walk's outward stage. Cross the stile alongside this to follow the fenced path beyond, past a right-hand paddock to a tree-lined descent to the footbridge over the Danes Stream which you previously crossed. Cross the stile beyond this to follow the right-hand side of a pasture to a gateway beyond which a fenced grass track leads you on ahead. After the track becomes gravelled, then metalled, you re-emerge past Danestream Farm Shop on to B3055, which you follow left-handed, with due care, for the final few hundred yards back to The Plough Inn at Tiptoe.

Alongside Christchurch Harbour and over Hengistbury Head

WALK 10
Allow 3 hours
5 miles
Walk begins page 60

Background to the Walk

Focusing upon one of the most scenic and popular recreational walking areas in the immediate neighbourhood of Christchurch and Bournemouth, this walk is also a journey into prehistory. Hengistbury Head, overlooking the broad spread of Christchurch Harbour in which the Dorset Stour and the Hampshire Avon unite before reaching the sea, is more than a mere promontory. As far back as the Bronze Age people recognised its value as a stronghold which could be readily defended as well as a landing place for vessels bringing merchandise from abroad. The sheltered anchorage offered by the water on the landward side and the view-commanding heights of the headland itself combined to offer unique advantages of which warring invaders and others made full use at different periods.

Hengistbury Head today is a place of peace. Footpaths wind their way over heathy heights where wayside seats invite you to pause and enjoy views without equal along this stretch of our southern shoreline. On breezy days a boisterous Channel contrasts with the calm, near-landlocked harbour in the opposite direction. In clear weather the seaward panorama extends from The Needles cliffs on the Isle of Wight, to your left, across to their Dorset mirror-image, thrusting out to Old Harry rock at The Foreland, south of Studland.

Inland, directly below you, Christchurch Harbour spreads like a lake. On its far side is Stanpit Marsh, a bird reserve of major importance, while the value of the near shoreline and its hinterland as a sanctuary

Maps
Landranger 1:50,000
Sheet 195
1:25,000
Outdoor Leisure 22, New Forest
Map Reference of Start/Finish SZ149922

How to get there
Your starting point, The Riverside pub at Tuckton, is situated alongside the River Stour halfway between Christchurch and Southbourne. From Southampton follow A3024 and then A35 around Totton and the New Forest and along Christchurch bypass. After skirting Christchurch proper turn left at the first traffic lights to follow B3059, Stour Road, half-a-mile along which, immediately after crossing the River Stour, you will see The Riverside pub on your right. From Bournemouth follow A35 (Christchurch Road) east to Iford roundabout, where you take the third exit to follow Iford Road, leading on via Iford Lane to join Tuckton Road, which you follow left to the first roundabout. Take the first exit and within a few yards you will reach The Riverside pub on your left. Trains from Southampton to Christchurch can be used to connect with Yellow Buses on services 22, 23, 25 or 68 from Christchurch town centre, all of which pass The Riverside pub at Tuckton

Bridge or stop within yards of it. In Bournemouth these buses serving Tuckton start from Gervis Place, near the Central Gardens.

Pub facilities
The Riverside

This Whitbread Brewer's Fayre pub has its own riverside garden on the south bank of the Dorset Stour and a large car park where pub-using walkers may leave their cars, but please ask first. (Alternative parking space is available alongside Wick Lane, the first road that turns left after crossing the Stour from the Christchurch direction.) Opening hours are 1100-2300 on weekdays and 1200-2230 on Sundays, food ordering times being from 1130 (from 1200 on Sundays) until 2200. Real ales include Flower's Original and Wadworth 6X and Greene King's Abbott. Murphy's Irish Stout, Guinness, and Strongbow and Woodpecker ciders are also on draught. Menu specialities include home made soup, egg mayonnaise, beef and lamb pie, cauliflower cheese, seafood lasagne, brunch grills, and breaded lemon sole served with chips or new potatoes or vegetables and salad. Among other dishes featured are vegetable lasagne, mushroom and nut fetuccini, and beef and ale pie. Daily specials are listed on a board. Separate bars for smokers and non-smokers, brick alcoves with upholstered seats and tables, and leadlight windows looking out on to the river are other features, and a new two-tier wooden patio overlooking the river has recently been added. The telephone number is 01202 429210.

The Riverside, Tuckton

for wild nature is also of a very high order. The headland itself is where many summer bird visitors to this country first make landfall after crossing the English Channel and where they gather before departure in the autumn, when the possibility of obtaining a glimpse of rare species is always present.

Where the combined waters of the Stour and the Avon reach the sea between Hengistbury Head and Mudeford is the tide-race called The Run. There licensed fishermen spread their nets in due season to harvest some of the salmon which enter the harbour on their way upriver to spawn. Inland, just beyond where the rivers which feed the harbour merge, Christchurch Priory Church stands proud above a scene it has dominated for the past 800 years. Near by is the Norman castle of the town anciently called Twynham from its situation between two rivers and, little less prominent, waterfront buildings which owe nothing to antiquity and everything to what has been deemed architecturally appropriate to one of the oldest towns in Wessex by 20th century planners and builders.

Walk 10

Distance: *Allow 3 hours for this 5-mile walk.*
From The Riverside pub at Tuckton cross adjacent

Stour Road to follow a macadamised path through a boatyard opposite. This leads to the south bank of the Stour, an inlet of which you skirt to follow a gravel path through tree-dotted pleasure grounds adjoining the boat covered river. Where a path continues ahead cross a wooden footbridge on your left and carry on along the river bank to where the gravel path ends.

Now continue across the grass ahead to where River House and its private grounds confront you at a point where you bear right, away from the river, to a resumed gravel path which follows a fenced course between two kissing-gates. Beyond the second of these gates your path bears right of a marshy pasture, with gravel giving way to grass as you follow the leftward edge of the next pasture to another kissing-gate. A signpost reminds you that you are on part of the Stour Way long-distance walk as you now follow a raised gravel path across a field to a wooden footbridge over a reedy water channel. Christchurch Priory looms beyond the river to your left as you now pass through another kissing-gate to enter Hengistbury Head Nature Reserve, a nationally important feeding and resting area for migrant birds.

Here your path, no longer gravelled, bears diagonally right to cross an area of rough grass dotted with brambles, bushes and gorse clumps with a wooden fence to your right. After passing through the next kissing-gate you repeat the process, angling right, away from the left-hand fence, beyond which are the reed-margined upper reaches of Christchurch Harbour. You now head for another kissing-gate where you emerge on to a tarmac drive leading to Hengistbury Outdoor Education and Field Study Centre, the green-roofed building on your left.

Cross the metalled driveway just to the right of the entrance gate to the field study centre to follow a path through a gorsy area and emerge on to another metalled road, which you follow ahead. The compound surrounding the thatched buildings to your right here serves as a stable for the road-train which offers the sole means of wheeled access to the beach chalets opposite Mudeford, at the eastern end of the headland. This shuttles to and fro throughout the day in the holiday season and at other times when public demand requires it.

Alongside the road you now follow is a seat facing the harbour: an ideal place to pause for a preliminary spy to see what birds may be in evidence. Crows and mallard, Britain's most common wild duck, were species most conspicuous on the day when we did this walk, but there is always an excellent chance of something extra special.

Follow the road to where it bends right into a wood. Just beyond this point you branch off to follow a gravel path left-ahead through scrub oaks and over rough pasture with the harbour to your left. The path then winds through some dense vegetation before converging with the harbour shore, or you can bypass this bushy section by taking a minor side-path to the left and then walking along the shore itself. Where a discernible footpath ends continue along the harbour's shingly shore to where a path presently resumes. A wooden footbridge takes you across a creek which snakes in from the harbour. Oyster catchers along the tideline took little notice of our passing as we continued to where the path rejoins the metalled road at the turnaround point for the road-train by the beach chalets which line the sandy shore here.

The River Stour at Tuckton

Follow the road right-handed to where it soon bends right, then go left-ahead along a footway beside the chalets to climb a stepped path to the higher ground of Hengistbury Head. At the top is a seat from which you can look back across the harbour-mouth to Mudeford, beyond which Highcliffe Castle peeps out above the clifftop. A guest here in Edwardian times was Germany's Kaiser Wilhelm II. During his stay he attended Sunday service at Christchurch Priory, in which a notice preserved to this day advised the regular congregation how to comport themselves in the awe-inspiring presence of H. I. M.

Where the high ground path soon triplicates follow the left-hand gravel path. A fence to the left of this marks the limit of safe movement where cliff erosion has been attacking the once solid soil of the upper headland. A small lake lies in a declivity to your right as you carry on up to a crossing of tracks where you turn left to pass a lookout station of H.M. Coastguard, which was closed and boarded-up when the author and a co-walker last saw it. A seat just beyond this, on your right, gives a grandstand view across the harbour where, on a summer's day, pleasure craft ceaselessly make their way to and from the open Channel. In the holiday season, too, a ferry operates between Christchurch and the harbour mouth opposite Mudeford, across which another ferry gives access to and from the Hengistbury side of The Run.

The path becomes metalled, then stepped, descending steeply as you follow it towards where you bear left to follow a wide coast path to the south end of Double Dykes, a 2,000-year-old Celtic earthwork protecting the western approach to the headland. A notice reminds us how laboriously this must have been constructed by an army of men using hand tools and baskets to dig and carry the soil, with some assistance from ox-wagons for the heavier haulage involved.

Turn right to follow a path alongside this earthwork to the metalled road used

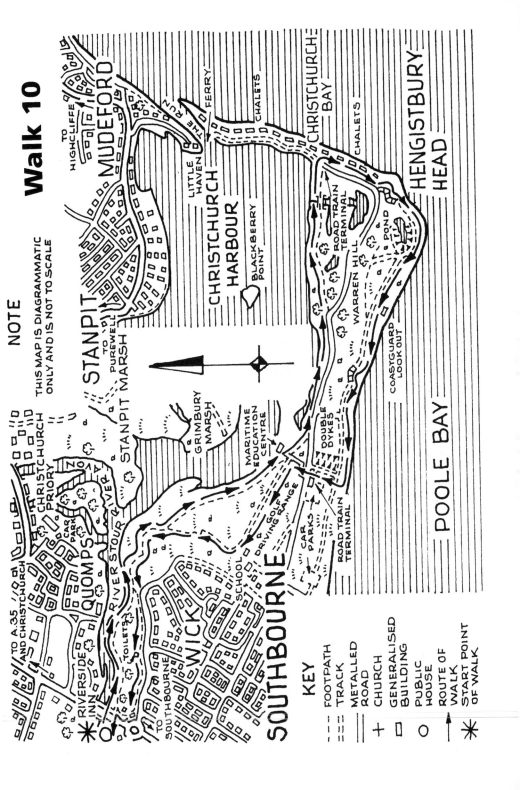

Walk 10

NOTE

THIS MAP IS DIAGRAMMATIC ONLY AND IS NOT TO SCALE

MUDEFORD

TO HIGHCLIFFE

THE RUN

FERRY

LITTLE HAVEN

CHALETS

CHRISTCHURCH BAY

CHALETS

HENGISTBURY HEAD

STANPIT

TO PUREWELL

STANPIT MARSH

CHRISTCHURCH HARBOUR

BLACKBERRY POINT

ROAD TRAIN TERMINAL

WARREN HILL

POND

COASTGUARD LOOK OUT

POOLE BAY

GRIMBURY MARSH

MARITIME EDUCATION CENTRE

DOUBLE DYKES

TO A.35 AND CHRISTCHURCH

RIVERSIDE INN

CHRISTCHURCH PRIORY

CAR PARK

QUOMPS

RIVER STOUR

AVON

TOILETS

WICK

SOUTHBOURNE

SCHOOL

DRIVING GOLF RANGE

CAR PARKS

ROAD TRAIN TERMINAL

TO SOUTHBOURNE

KEY

- - - FOOTPATH

≡≡≡ TRACK

——— METALLED ROAD

+ CHURCH

▢ GENERALISED BUILDING

○ PUBLIC HOUSE

→ ROUTE OF WALK

✳ START POINT OF WALK

Near Hengistbury Head

by the road-train. Cross this to join and follow a narrow road to the near side of the gateway to Hengistbury Field Study Centre. Here you turn left around the first of two gates on that side to follow a semi-derelict metalled track, with a golf course to your left and a wooden fence to your right. When you reach a scissors-crossing of tracks continue towards a building left-ahead (Solent Coffee Shop, 'open all day'), from which you turn right to a kissing-gate. Pass through this to follow a path along the leftward edge of rough pasture with a fence on your left-hand side.

Go left through the next kissing-gate to cross a marshy, sluggish stream by a concrete bridge and then immediately turn right to cross a plank bridge over a ditch. You now bear left to follow a narrow path between bushes on your right and the ditch to your left, emerging from which your path angles right in line with Christchurch Priory, ahead, before twisting left and then right through a kissing-gate to join and follow left-handed the raised gravel path you followed on the outward stage of the walk. Gravel ceases as you enter the next field, the right-hand edge of which you follow to where a gravelled way resumes and curves left as a fenced path between kissing-gates.

Emerging just left of River House and to the right of Wick Farm and its buildings, cross the riverside recreation ground to follow the river-bank path left-handed. Where this path fairly soon divides keep left to follow a metalled footpath along the left-hand edge of the timbered pleasure ground. After skirting right of a public convenience and to the left of an ice-cream sales booth you will emerge past the boatyard first encountered on to Stour Road, which you cross to retrieve your car from The Riverside pub car park.

Paths and Green Lanes near Sopley

WALK 11
At least 3 hours
5 miles
Walk begins page 67

Background to the Walk

Until late Saxon times the countryside extending all the way from The Weald, in Kent, Surrey and Sussex, across Hampshire and well into Dorset was almost continuous forest. The New Forest, as we now know it, had yet to be named. The larger wasteland of which it formed part was called Ytene, supposedly meaning 'the country of the Jutes', which suggests that Jutes, rather than Saxons, originally wrested much of it from its native British inhabitants and established their settlements in it.

These would have necessitated clearings in the forest which were identified in placenames by the common suffix 'ley' (Old English 'leah'). Recorded in Domesday Book as 'Sopelie', the village name Sopley probably originated to define a forest clearing owned by a man called Soppa. On the other hand, 'soppa' was apparently an Old English word meaning 'marsh', so perhaps the clearing was merely a moist one. This would hardly be surprising, for the countryside hereabouts is very flat and the River Avon, famously flood-prone — in winter especially — flows close by.

This early, forest-fringed settlement undoubtedly had a church: a wooden structure in the first instance, and almost certainly located on the slight eminence where stands the Church of St Michael and All Angels, serving the parish of Sopley today. Begun in the 13th century, the squat-towered, stone-walled building contains several sculptures of that period or perhaps of the 14th century. The usual memorials to leading local families are in evidence. One such

Maps
Landranger 1:50,000
Sheet 195
1:25,000
Outdoor Leisure 22, New Forest
Map Reference of Start/Finish
SZ157969

How to get there
Sopley lies just over 3 miles north of Christchurch on B3347, the old, direct main road between Ringwood and Christchurch. From Southampton head west along A3024 and then along A35 around Lyndhurst, via Holmsley and along Christchurch bypass, which you follow as far as a roundabout where you take the third exit to head north along B3347 past Burton and via Winkton to Sopley, the next village, where The Woolpack lies on your right. From Bournemouth follow Wessex Way to Cooper Dean roundabout where you filter left to take the third exit, A3060. At the next roundabout bear left to follow A35 around Christchurch and for a short distance along Christchurch bypass before turning left to follow B3347 north, as directed above. Buses on Solent Blue Line/Wilts & Dorset services X1, X2 and X5 from Southampton connect at Ringwood with Wilts & Dorset service 125 which calls at Sopley en route to

Christchurch. From Bournemouth, Yellow Buses on services 20, 22, 23, 25, 68 and, by indirect routes, 31 and 32, all run to Christchurch High Street, from which Wilts & Dorset buses on service 125 call at Sopley.

Pub facilities
The Woolpack, Sopley
Open all day on weekdays from 1100-2300 and on Sundays from 1200-2230, this very popular pub, which dates from the 17th century and was once a coaching inn, takes food orders between 1200-1430 and 1830-2130 (from 1900 on Sundays) seven days a week. Real ales include Ringwood Bitter and Wadworth 6X. Also on draught are IPA Bitter, Guinness, Murphy's Irish stout and Black-Jack cider. The lunch menu will tempt you with dishes such as salmon in white wine, turkey breast with port and apricot sauce, haddock and prawn Florentine, lamb noisettes in a dijonnaise sauce, half a roast chicken with apricot stuffing, cod and broccoli au gratin, rainbow trout and prawns in lemon butter sauce, braised steak in red wine, onions and cream, all served with vegetables and potatoes, or a choice of 4 salads, Daily specials might feature, say, whole fresh Mudeford lobster or fresh mussels in white wine, garlic and cream with granary bread. There is also a good choice of desserts. Children are admitted except in the bar area. You will find no fruit machines or jukebox, but as well as background music there is a self-playing electronic piano performing music arranged by Caroline on Thursday evenings. Two open fires enhance winter comfort. The pub garden overlooks a substantial brook with a large complement of ducks. The large

The Woolpack, Sopley

family, named Willis, owned adjacent Sopley Park and supplied two vicars to add to a list of known incumbents dating back to 1308.

More recent items of special interest include a model Vietnamese fishing-boat. This was made and given as a token of gratitude for local hospitality by refugee boat people from that corner of south-east Asia, 600 of whom were accommodated for a time in the old RAF camp on the Bransgore side of Sopley after arriving in England in 1979. Another handsome church embellishment is a 1984 tapestry with Sopley as its subject.

Sopley Mill, just behind the church, has a history stretching back over many centuries. Water from the mill stream still flushes vigorously through it but has long since ceased to turn a mill-wheel. It provides a pleasing visual adjunct to premises which now function as a fashionable restaurant.

Sopley's old world cottages include a number of thatched ones and crowd close to a narrow main road which now forms part of a one-way traffic system through the village. The Woolpack itself is thatched and lies in the 'island' created by the modern through traffic arrangements. A second village pub was closed down years ago and is now a private dwelling, but Sopley is still the lucky possessor of a village stores and post office.

car park fills up quickly at weekends, and walkers using the pub should ask first before leaving their cars there. The telephone number is 01425 672252.

The Church of St Michael and All Saints

Walk 11

Distance: *Allow at least 3 hours for this five mile walk.*
From The Woolpack head south for a few yards to the junction where the one way traffic system reunites towards the Christchurch end of Sopley and there turn right to follow a short cul-de-sac for a look at the ruggedly stone-built Church of St Michael and All Angels. If there are problems about parking your car at the pub while doing the walk there is alternative space near here and elsewhere in Sopley. Just behind and below the church is Sopley Mill, now revamped as a restaurant specialising in four-course dinners. The water rushing beneath it is a sidestream of the Avon, whose many-channelled course spreads across a half-mile width and more of the flat land west of Sopley.

After this short initial digression walk back to the main road and follow it left, past The Woolpack once more and so northward past the village stores and post office, on your left. If you want to learn more about local lore than I have sketched out by way of introducing the setting for this walk, a local author has published a village history which is on sale here.

Not many yards farther on a sign points out where The Avon Valley Path turns off right-handed. This relatively new long-distance walk linking Christchurch and Salisbury passes through Sopley village centre before resuming a footpath course here, where you cross a stile and head north with a hedgerow to your left and a picturesque tree-bordered brook to your right. This brook is the selfsame one which flows through the garden of The Woolpack. It has its source in the New Forest, among the moors and oozy bogs which sprawl on the Ringwood side of Burley, and by the time it reaches Sopley it has grown to a mini-river which then spills into the Avon.

A second stile precedes a field, the right-hand edge of which you follow to a

The brookside path near Sopley

third stile, which you cross to follow a fenced path to a fourth stile. This served as a seat near the grass-bordered brook for a picnic lunch enjoyed in sunshine after a shower on the autumn day when we tried this walk. While keeping a weather eye well open for more rainclouds — none materialised — we were glad of the comforting proximity of the oaks.

Not many yards farther on a wicket-gate leads out on to a narrow country lane. The Avon Valley Path follows this leftward, but you cross it to follow another signposted brookside path through trees. This leads ahead to a stile around which you walk to follow the right-hand edge of an arable field. You then head through more trees to emerge on to another lane, which you cross to follow a path over a stile and along the right-hand margin of another arable field. Towards the far end of this your path heads into streamside oaks to your right to join another path at right-angles to your own.

Follow this right-handed over a stream bridge, a short distance beyond which your new path becomes a lane. This leads past houses to a T-junction of lanes at the northern end of Ripley. Here you angle left to cross the lane ahead and pass through a wicket-gate to follow a hedged green lane. Signposted as a footpath, this follows a fairly straight course in an easterly direction. Mature trees to your left contrast with newly planted ones to your right for a few hundred yards until taller wayside timber flanks your route on that side also.

A plank bridge over a small stream is followed soon by a gate with a notice: 'horse riding prohibited'. Beyond this you pass a galvanised iron building set back into woodland on your left and join a gravel lane which you follow right-handed to another gate preceding a metalled lane.

Follow the lane left-handed for a few yards to where it forks, and here bear right. Within a few more yards a signposted, well-used footpath leads you right-handed through trees to a stile. After crossing this you follow the right-

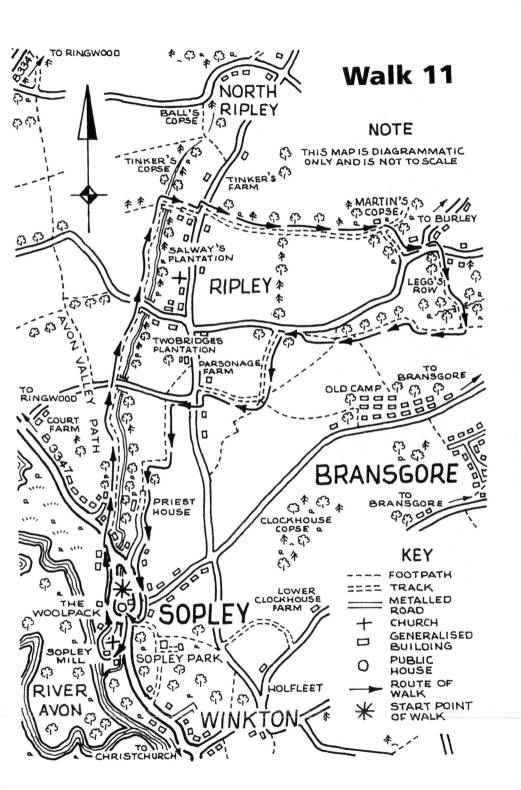

Walk 11

NOTE

THIS MAP IS DIAGRAMMATIC ONLY AND IS NOT TO SCALE

TO RINGWOOD

B3347

NORTH RIPLEY

BALL'S COPSE

TINKER'S COPSE

TINKER'S FARM

MARTIN'S COPSE

TO BURLEY

SALWAY'S PLANTATION

RIPLEY

LEGG'S ROW

AVON VALLEY PATH

TWO BRIDGES PLANTATION

PARSONAGE FARM

OLD CAMP

TO BRANSGORE

TO RINGWOOD

COURT FARM

B3347

PRIEST HOUSE

BRANSGORE

TO BRANSGORE

CLOCKHOUSE COPSE

THE WOOLPACK

SOPLEY

LOWER CLOCKHOUSE FARM

SOPLEY MILL

SOPLEY PARK

HOLFLEET

RIVER AVON

WINKTON

TO CHRISTCHURCH

KEY

- - - - FOOTPATH

==== TRACK

—— METALLED ROAD

✝ CHURCH

▢ GENERALISED BUILDING

◯ PUBLIC HOUSE

→ ROUTE OF WALK

✳ START POINT OF WALK

Sopley village

hand edge of a pasture, bearing left with it at the far end to reach and cross a plank bridge over a stream followed by a stile a few yards to your right. Follow the right-hand edge of the next pasture to a stile by another footpath sign, on your right. Crossing this, with houses on the edge of Bransgore visible just beyond trees to your left, you now follow a well-defined path along the right-hand edge of a meadow, with an oak-bordered stream directly to your right.

Three further stiles with intervening pastures precede a woody footpath section. Along this a low stile precedes in its turn a handrailed footbridge over a brook and a further stile, beyond which a clear path follows the right-hand edge of an arable field. A gap through a hedge leads into a further arable field, midway along the right-hand edge of which you cross a stile on your right to emerge on to a narrow metalled lane. Follow this left-handed for perhaps 150 yards before turning left to follow a hedged green lane signposted as a byway.

Where this latter joins a field-access track emerging from your left, the two combined swing right. The hedged track you now follow becomes metalled just before joining a metalled lane, which you follow left-handed for a few yards before turning right to follow another hedged lane. Carry on along this metalled byway as far as a slight bend to the right where you cross a stile on your left. A wide unploughed headland forms your path along the left-hand side of an arable field, with a high-fenced grass field to your left. At the field's far end your path bends right with it to the far corner from where you first entered the field, where you cross a stile on your left.

You now follow a hedged path with overhanging trees which soon becomes a green lane. This is turn becomes metalled as you pass 17th century Priest House on your right, beyond which you carry on ahead to reach the main road once more in Sopley. Turn left here and then circle right to find your way back to The Woolpack and its car park, or to the cul-de-sac which leads to the church, if that is where you left your car.

Footpaths and Forest near Ringwood

WALK 12
Allow 3 hours
5 ¼ miles
Walk begins page 73

Background to the Walk

The Avon Valley town of Ringwood was a royal manor in Saxon times, when it already had a church as well as a mill. In AD955 it was recorded as 'Rimucwuda', which probably meant 'a wood on a boundary'. Just which boundary this was one can only guess: certainly not that of the New Forest, as at present, because until William I 'created' it in or about the year 1079 the Forest did not exist as such but was part of a much larger semi-wilderness called 'Ytene'.

Few Saxon places of worship long survived the zeal for building new churches which swept the country in Norman times and later. Ringwood gained a new church of its own in the 13th century. Much added to and altered by later 'restorers', this was demolished and replaced by another new structure, the present one, in the 19th century. A secular Ringwood building of some interest is a pub just off the A31, The Original White Hart. This refers to a white hart, or stag, called Albert, which is supposed to have been set free in the New Forest to provide a quarry for hunting one day when Henry VII was present. The hunt went ahead as planned. Albert performed so well that when at last he would run no farther he was caught up in the watermeadows beside the Avon, just outside Ringwood, and adorned with a gold crown around his neck, thereafter to lead a charmed existence. Ringwood's White Hart pub and others up and down the country use a white stag likewise embellished as the centrepiece of their sign.

Perhaps Henry VII recalled an incident involving another white hart, this time in Blackmoor Forest,

Maps
Landranger 1:50,000
Sheet 195
1:25,000
Outdoor Leisure 22, New Forest
Map Reference of Start/Finish
SU163048

How to get there
The Elm Tree Inn lies at the junction of Hightown Road and Crow Lane, on the south-eastern edge of Ringwood. If heading west along A31, having reached this via A3024, M271 and M27 from the Southampton direction, take the first turning left after passing the turn-off for Burley at Picket Post and you will reach the starting-point pub after about a mile-and-a-half, on your right. If approaching from the west or from Bournemouth via Wessex Way and A338, take the Ringwood town centre exit from the interchange where A338 from Salisbury joins A31 and follow B3347 for just over half-a-mile towards the southern end of Ringwood before turning left just short of the site of Ringwood's old railway station to follow Hightown Road. When you soon reach a T-junction with Eastfield Lane, turn right to carry on along Hightown Road for a very short distance before The Elm Tree appears on your left. Buses on Solent Blue Line/Wilts & Dorset services X1, X2 and X5

between Southampton and Bournemouth and Wilts & Dorset service X3 between Poole, Bournemouth and Salisbury connect at Ringwood with local buses on Wilts & Dorset services 136 and 137, which pass along Eastfield Lane, with a stop just round the corner from the pub.

Pub facilities
The Elm Tree Inn
Open all day from 1100-2300 on weekdays and from 1200-2230 on Sundays, this picturesque thatched pub with its inglenook fireplace, beams and exposed brickwork is a grade two listed building. Originally a dairy farm, it became a pub in the 1970s. The elm tree after which it was named has vanished, like so many others. Separate bar and restaurant menus are complemented by a very good range of blackboard specials, which are changed at frequent intervals. The regular restaurant menu offers a choice of seven starters ranging from chef's soup of the day, lemon battered prawns and garlic mushrooms to potato skins with various fillings. Old favourites include steak and kidney pie, or you may opt for chilli con carne, chicken tikka masala or Cajun chicken. Fish dishes include whole fillet of breaded plaice, breaded haddock and salmon steak. Pasta Bolognese or lasagne may also tempt you, or perhaps rump or sirloin steak, lamb cutlets or gammon. Mixed grills and lunchtimes specials such as baguettes and jacket potatoes are other options as well as salads, ploughman's, vegetarian dishes and various 'side extras'. Sunday roasts, hot puddings, sundaes and ice creams of three different flavours are on offer and there is a special children's menu. To

The Elm Tree in Hightown Road

north Dorset, where Henry III was hunting when a stag of this colour appeared in front of hounds. When this stag was killed by others a short time afterwards the King ordered fines and imprisonment of those responsible and imposed a special land tax which continued for generations. The village of Kingstag in Blackmoor Vale marks the scene of this sad occurrence.

You just might see deer in the New Forest corner explored on this walk, but the odds are against it due to the area's popularity with walkers, who cause inevitable disturbance. You are even less likely to see a white deer, though if you do it will be a fallow deer buck, not a hart: a term confined to prime males of the red deer species, be they red in colour or otherwise.

This walk affords plenty of variety: Forest-edge farmland, hilly heathland, timberland tranquillity, sleepy suburbia — and a lake beloved of geese whose forebears came to this country from Canada and are now very much at home here. A name shared with a species of bird much in evidence in these parts is that of the Forest-fringe hamlet called Crow, where you glimpse the remnants of a railway along which express trains once ran between London, Southampton and Dorchester but which was axed by Dr Beeching in his purge of the 1960s.

Walk 12

Distance: *Allow at least 3 hours for this five-and-a-quarter mile walk.*

Leaving The Elm Tree behind you on your left, immediately go through a walk-through stile on your left, next to the pub, to follow where a footpath sign points diagonally right-handed across a pasture sub-divided for grazing purposes by electric fencing. The footpath's route is waymarked through successive gaps in this fencing wide enough for walkers but not for farm livestock. This brings you to a footbridge over a stream with a stile on its far side, which you cross to follow a waymarked route to a stile in a right-hand hedge. After crossing this you follow the right-hand hedge of an oblong meadow to reach a stile leading out on to a lane.

Head left along this lane for a very few yards before following a hedged gravel track diagonally right from the metalled byway. Signposted as a bridleway, the gravel track meanders steadily uphill between scattered dwellings very much of the 'des res' category one would expect of a Forest-edge suburb like this one, Hightown, of an old country town like Ringwood. Tucked away in their own private woodland sanctuaries, some of these houses have driveways which might briefly lead you astray from the arterial gravel track you should be following, but such a mistake will quickly be realised. After about three-quarters of a mile you reach and cross a metalled road to walk through a gate alongside a cattlegrid and enter the Forest itself.

You now head diagonally right from the road just crossed to follow another gravel track. This leads through scattered oaks and bracken with more 'des res' dwellings on your right, soon reaching a crossing of tracks where you continue left-ahead, with a fence at first on your right and then brackeny open forest on both sides. Next you join and follow right-ahead a semi-metalled road serving Forest-edge houses. Gravel soon reasserts itself, and at the approach to a house where your gravel track divides, fork left.

Not many yards past a left-hand tennis court and houses called White Lodge and Foulford Lodge the gravel track ends, and two low posts on your right mark the start of a footpath which you follow. Within a few yards you reach a crossing-point of five paths. Bear half-right here to follow a path which heads south-east across a moorland mixture of heather, fern and gorse. Having climbed this far from the Avon Valley, you can now look across it from high, open ground to where the hazy Purbeck Hills loom on the distant Dorset skyline, well on the other side of Bournemouth.

accompany your meal you can choose from an excellent range of white, rose, red or Spanish wines, or perhaps a bottle of champagne to celebrate a special occasion. Brews on draught include Wadworth 6X, Flower's Original, Fuller's London Pride and a guest ale as well as Heineken, Heineken Export and Stella lagers. Murphy's stout, Whitbread Best Bitter and Strongbow dry cider are also on draught here. Food ordering times are 1200-1430 and 1800-2100 (until 2130 on Fridays and Saturdays). An adjacent former barn has been adapted as a function room for wedding receptions and similar events and is also used as a skittle alley. Walkers using the pub may use the pub car park. The telephone number is 01425 472516.

Your gravelly path winds down into Foulford Bottom to cross a stream there by a footbridge. Forest streams tend to be dark and well-supplied with aquatic wildlife, and this one is no exception. Pond-skaters were light-footedly walking the water when we passed.

Your path now climbs a shoulder of moorland to reach a crossing of tracks quite close to a forest car park on your left. Turn right here to follow a wide grass-and-gravel track which heads south-west along a gorse-grown ridge crest. The route you are now following was probably one of several in these parts once used by smugglers. In the heart of Ridley Wood, near by, is an ancient hollow lane which is supposed to have been a meeting-point for traffickers in contraband brandy landed under cover of darkness after being shipped across from France.

Castle Hill, a moorland vantage point west of Burley, rears to your left as you approach the end of the view-commanding moorland ridge, having kept left-ahead at a fork of tracks where a gravel track bears right. Your track descends to join a road by scattered pine trees. Follow this road right-ahead for a very few yards before turning right to follow a fairly well-defined path along a grassy strip with a Forest-edge fence to your left. Within a quarter-of-a-mile this path skirts a cluster of birch and pine trees to form a T-junction with a path which you follow left to a gate adjoined by a stile.

Cross the stile to follow a fenced path to a metal gate, through which you pass to follow another fenced section of footpath. This brings you to a stile where a footpath sign points the way ahead, half-left across a lawned expanse, downhill to bridge a brook just below an ornamental pond to join a gravel driveway serving a timber-framed house called St. Andrew's Lodge.

Hurn Farm and other sizeable houses in secluded grounds flank the tree-bordered driveway you now follow left-handed. Heading north-westward, this crosses again the stream you previously crossed in Foulford Bottom. Sometimes macadamised, sometimes not, the drive heads uphill to a bend, with a wood beyond, where you turn left with it. A subsequent bend to the right precedes another, to the left, a few yards beyond which, having disregarded a previous leftward-pointing footpath sign, you turn left and leave this driveway to follow another along which a public footpath sign points.

Where this latter gravel drive soon ends, cross a stile left-ahead of you here, followed by two walk-through stiles between sections of a wooden-railed horse paddock, across which you head diagonally left-handed. Here you come close to the Foulford brook once again after crossing another stile to follow a fenced path with a tree-bordered stream gully to your left. From this you emerge past a large agricultural building to skirt left of housing development. Walk around the next stile to carry on along the path ahead, with the tree-shaded Foulford stream in its gully still directly to your left.

The stream bypasses a largish lake on the site of former gravel workings, with wooded islands in its middle and, when we passed, a sizeable gaggle of

Walk 12

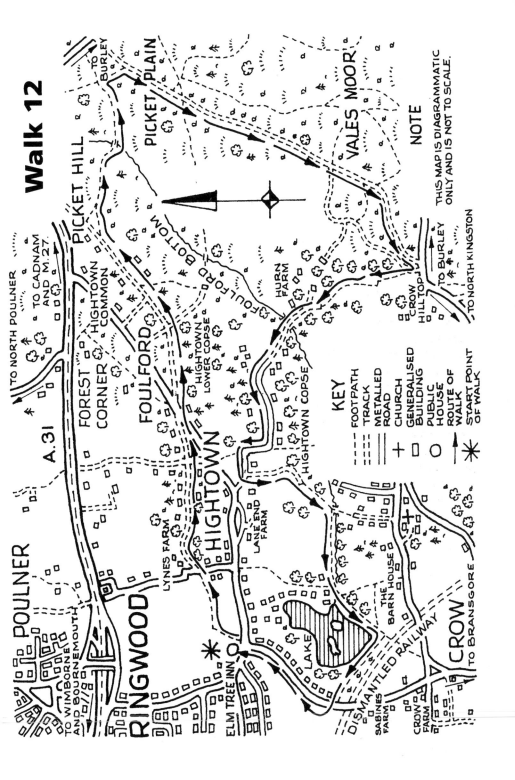

POULNER

A.31

TO NORTH POULNER

TO CADNAM AND M.27

FOREST CORNER

PICKET HILL

TO BURLEY

PICKET PLAIN

VALES MOOR

NOTE

THIS MAP IS DIAGRAMMATIC ONLY AND IS NOT TO SCALE.

HIGHTOWN COMMON

FOULFORD BOTTOM

HURN FARM

HIGHTOWN LOWER COPSE

CROW HILL TOP

TO BURLEY

TO NORTH KINGSTON

FOULFORD

TO WIMBORNE AND BOURNEMOUTH

RINGWOOD

LYNES FARM

HIGHTOWN

LANE END FARM

HIGHTOWN COPSE

KEY

FOOTPATH

TRACK

METALLED ROAD

CHURCH

GENERALISED BUILDING

PUBLIC HOUSE

ROUTE OF WALK

START POINT OF WALK

ELM TREE INN

LAKE

THE BARN HOUSE

SABINES FARM

DISMANTLED RAILWAY

CROW FARM

CROW

TO BRANSGORE

The tree-fringed lake near Crow

constantly honking Canada geese. We saw an even larger flock of these geese enjoying a meal of lush meadow grass in one of the pastures to our left as we followed the path along the east bank of the lake, at the end of which the lakeside path turns sharply right. Leaving the lake behind you on your right, you cross a stile to follow the left-hand edge of a sheep pasture. A metal gate precedes a further pasture, at the end of which you cross another stile. Your path now continues across some waste ground choked in summer with vegetation and flanked by gardens to the right, leading to a final stile where you join Crow Lane and follow this to the right.

To avoid the stiles and the rank vegetation, instead of turning immediately right to follow the path along the south bank of the lake you can carry on for a further yard or two to join and follow right-handed the parallel course of what you may now hardly recognise as the old Southampton-Dorchester railway. The derelict stretch of it in question once ran from Brockenhurst via Ringwood and Wimborne to merge with the present Bournemouth route at Hamworthy Junction, west of Poole. Known as Castleman's Corkscrew after the Wimborne solicitor who connived its tortuous route to bypass the heart of the New Forest while also serving his home town, this was closed in the 1960s as part of the railway rationalisation instigated by Dr. Beeching when he was chairman of British Rail.

Having emerged directly opposite where Crow Arch Lane diverges west, turn right and follow Crow Lane north for a quarter-of-a-mile to where The Elm Tree beckons ahead, facing Crow Lane's junction with Hightown Road.

Avon Valley Paths Around Ibsley

WALK 13
At least 4 hours
7 miles
Walk begins page 78

Background to the Walk

Ibsley is one of those places where the term 'old' has special meaning. The little Avon Valley village already existed when William the Conqueror was rubbing in the fact of his conquest by having a detailed inventory taken of what he had gained through winning the Battle of Hastings. In his Domesday survey it featured as 'Tibeslei', meaning 'woodland clearing of a man called Tibbi or Ibbi', a personal name known from other evidence to have been in use at that time. Two hundred years later it was recorded afresh as 'Ibeslehe'.

Most of Ibsley's dwellings today are strikingly redolent of antiquity. Times past are reflected in house names: The Old Rectory, The Old Bailiff's House, The Old Smithy, The Old Post Office — each a reminder of departed village vitality as a self-dependent working community. Ibsley today, like many another small country village, slumbers as peacefully as the traffic streaming through it will permit, with the pub, and little else, as a surviving hub of activity. Even the little church, built in 1832, is now closed.

The three-arched bridge across the Avon here is robust and enduring, which is just as well in view of its being the only public means of crossing the river on wheels between Ringwood and Fordingbridge.

Beyond the Avon looms Harbridge church, which was built in 1838 though the tower is older and conspicuous not just as the dominating feature in an otherwise level landscape but because of the stair turret which surmounts it. The prefix 'Har' in 'Harbridge' perhaps derives from the Old English

Maps
Landranger 1:50,000
Sheet 195
1:25,000
Outdoor Leisure 22, New Forest
Map Reference of Start/Finish
SU150093

How to get there
Ibsley is on A338 halfway between Fordingbridge and Ringwood. From Southampton follow A3024, M271 and westbound M27 to Cadnam, B3079 to Brook, B3078 from there to Fordingbridge and southbound A338 from there to Ibsley, where The Old Beams is on your left, or follow A3024, M271, westbound M27 and A31 to Ringwood and northbound A338 from there to Ibsley. Leave Bournemouth via Wessex Way to follow A338 to Ringwood, briefly joining A31 here before resuming A338 to Ibsley. Solent Blue Line/Wilts & Dorset buses on services X1, X2 and X5 from Southampton connect at Ringwood with Wilts & Dorset service X3 between Poole, Bournemouth and Salisbury, which pass through Ibsley.

Pub facilities
The Old Beams, Ibsley.
A spectacularly ancient confection of thatch and knobbly beams draws the eye of passers-by unfailingly to this free house on the east side of the busy A338, though as a pub it

is not all that old. What had been just a pair of pretty cottages became a tearoom in World War II. Proceed either to the restaurant or to the main, self-service bar with its mouth-watering array of viands laid out for you to see. Weekday opening hours are 1100–1500 and 1800-2300, Sunday hours being 1100 (1200 for bar facilities)-1500 and 1830-2230 and food may be ordered between 1200-1345 and 1900-2115 seven days a week. At busy times food may be ordered up to half an hour or so later than the above times at lunchtimes and in the evenings. Menu items range from roast of the day, home made steak and kidney pie with vegetables and potatoes, curried beef and turkey, to rump, sirloin and fillet steaks from best Scotch beef, turkey and bacon pie, smoked trout or mackerel, not forgetting various cold meats, ploughman's, sandwiches and hot meat roll. Real ales include Bishop's Tipple, Old Thumper, Royal Oak, Burton, Wadworth 6X, Ringwood Best Bitter and HSB. There is a rear garden and a large rear car park which pub-using walkers may use. Parties of walkers are regularly catered for and table reservations for larger parties may be booked by telephoning 01425 473387.

The Royal Oak, North Gorley.
Open on weekdays from 1100-1430 (until 1500 on Saturdays) and from 1800-2300 and all day from 1200-2230 on Sundays, this charming thatched pub on a picturesque Forest-edge byway takes orders for food between 1200-1400 and 1830-2100 seven days a week. As well as five or six daily specials, roasts, chillis, curries and items like egg and

'heord' meaning herds or flocks and, hence, a crossing-place for farm livestock over the otherwise sparsely-bridged river. Bickton, a little way upstream, probably started as a placename to mark a farm holding by someone called Bica. North and South Gorley, east of the river, are typical small Forest-fringe villages complete with ponies and other denizens of the neighbouring wide open spaces.

Walk 13

Distance: *Allow 4 hours for this seven mile walk.*
Leaving The Old Beams behind you on your right, head north along the footway between A338 and a short succession of old cottages, then take care as you cross the busy highway to follow the road that heads west towards Harbridge. You immediately cross Ibsley Bridge and then turn left through a wicket-gate to follow a path across a meadow. Where the path divides the leftward spur is private. Here you bear right to follow what becomes a riverside path to the first of the many stiles you cross on this walk.

The river-edge path continues to the next stile, having crossed which you follow a clear path diverging right from the river to cross a meadow. Beyond the next stile carry on to a footbridge over an Avon sidestream with a stile on either side of it. Here you emerge on to a lane at the end of a metalled section where it turns right and becomes gravelled. Continue ahead along the hedged, unmetalled lane to where three dwellings including a farmhouse face a green with a reedy pond in it at the little hamlet of Turmer.

Turn right here, with the farmhouse to your left as you cross a stile to follow the left-hand edge of a pasture, with an open-sided thatched barn on your left-hand side behind the farmhouse. Beyond the next stile follow the tree-hedged leftward edge of another pasture to a further stile, beyond which you veer slightly right to cross a stile leading out on to a lane just west of Harbridge. Follow this left-handed past a bungalow and cottage on your left, at the hamlet of Kent, before turning where a footpath sign flanks a gap in the roadside hedge.

Although the footpath sign points straight ahead, the path itself turns right to follow the right-hand edge of an arable field to its far right corner, where a disused stile flanks another hedge-gap. Pass through this by one of the Avon's sidestreams to reach the end of a gravel lane with an isolated cottage to the right of it.

The gravel lane leads you left-handed past scattered thatched dwellings to join a metalled lane at Harbridge Green, directly opposite a partly thatched house with a tiled gable on which is a solar panel — an uncommon blend of ancient and modern.

Here, as elsewhere on the route thus far and for some little way yet to come, you are on The Avon Valley Path, a 34-mile walking route from Christchurch to Salisbury. Opened in 1992, this is well-signposted throughout, with an identifying logo in the form of a two-arched bridge to single it out from numerous intersecting paths. One of these signs directs you right-handed to follow the road here as far as a stile on your left, which you cross to follow a fenced path along the left-hand edge of a pasture. This leads to a footbridge over a stream and another stile, beyond which you head diagonally right and slightly uphill across another pasture to a stile in a fence a few yards left of a cottage garden. Cross this to follow the arrowed footpath route left-ahead across a grassy hump to a stile preceding a road.

Follow the road right-handed, then soon turn left by a footpath sign to follow a gated and fenced gravel farm track to a gap in a hedge right-ahead of this. Pass through this and turn right to follow the right-hand edge of a field to a boardwalk and footbridge across a minor arm of the Avon. Beyond these your path bends left, crossing two stiles and heading north along the left-hand edge of a pasture. When you reach the pasture's far left-hand corner follow the hedge here to your right to a stile on your left-hand side. After crossing this you follow the right-hand edge of a weedy pasture, bearing slightly right with the pasture's alignment to cross two stiles within feet of each other. Beyond these you follow a tree-lined, grass-centred gravelly track for a little way.

Cross the first stile on the left of this to cross rough ground to the next stile about 100 yards ahead. Cross this and continue ahead across the next pasture, veering right towards the end of it to cross a stile preceding a junction of public footpaths. Here you leave The Avon Valley Path, at least for the present, and turn right to bridge one of the Avon's lesser arms followed by a succession of minor sidestreams. Alongside a trout farm your path joins a track which you

chips, toasted sandwiches and ploughman's are Royal Oak regulars as well as fresh fish when available. Brews on tap include Ringwood Best Bitter, Fuller's London Pride, Wadworth 6X and Gale's HSB. Guinness, lagers, cider and wines are also on draught and coffee is always available. This is a popular social centre with a flourishing darts team and is a regular venue for guest cricketers. Morris dancers and the local Hyde brass band perform periodically in summer. Facilities include a beer garden, a family and games room. A friendly ghost called Hannah lives upstairs and is apt to be talkative. The oak which grows in front of the pub may not be royal, but is certainly ancient. The telephone number is 01425 652244.

The Royal Oak, North Gorley

follow right-handed across the main body of the river to Bickton Mill. Turn left to cross the mill-race and join a road which you follow right-handed into Bickton village.

Where this soon bends left and another lane bears half-right, follow the latter. As you approach where a house right-ahead of you faces the river across a lawn, turn left to follow a farm track through Bickton Farm. Leaving the farm buildings behind you on your right, follow a gravel track ahead, with a hedge soon on your left and a field to your right. When you reach a footpath sign on your right, head across the field in the direction indicated to reach and cross a stile on which is a prominent yellow disc marker.

This stile precedes the busy A338, which you cross — take care — to a stile directly opposite. Head across the field beyond this to a point just left of a right-angled bend in the hedge left-ahead, beyond the field. You emerge through a gap here on to a lane, which you follow right-handed for a few yards before turning right by a footpath sign to enter and cross a field on a route in alignment with where the sign points. Make for a gap in the hedge on the field's far side just to the right of a slight bend in it. After passing through it keep to the same straight alignment as before. Cross a stile directly ahead to follow an arrowed route half-right across a corner of a paddock to the next stile. Cross this and head for the next stile preceding a fenced path and another stile. Skirt right-handed of a bungalow to cross a final stile preceding the next road.

This you follow right-handed through North Gorley, with its pony-haunted green, its sometimes duck-thronged pond and its Royal Oak pub, a hostelry very much in keeping with its Forest-edge surroundings. The unfenced road leads on ahead to a point just past the first leftward turning, where you turn left just past Forge Cottage to follow a rather squelchy grass track fenced from neighbouring private property. This joins a gravel lane which you follow right-ahead, climbing fairly steeply to emerge past hill-slope paddocks and a dwelling on to the crest of Gorley Hill, with Gorley Common directly ahead.

Here turn fairly sharply right-handed to follow a path through bracken and scattered trees along the hill-crest, with views of the Avon across the low ground

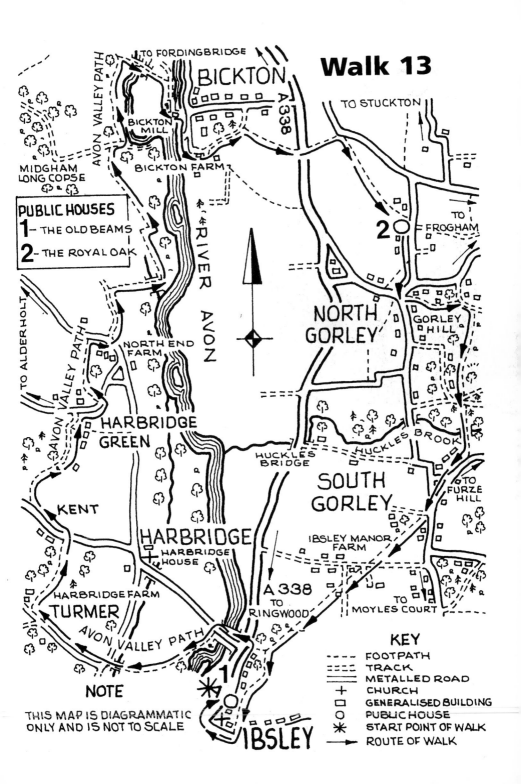

Walk 13

TO FORDINGBRIDGE

BICKTON

A 338

TO STUCKTON

AVON VALLEY PATH

BICKTON MILL

MIDGHAM LONG COPSE

BICKTON FARM

TO FROGHAM

2

PUBLIC HOUSES
1 — THE OLD BEAMS
2 — THE ROYAL OAK

TO ALDERHOLT

RIVER AVON

NORTH GORLEY

GORLEY HILL

AVON VALLEY PATH

NORTH END FARM

HARBRIDGE GREEN

HUCKLES BROOK

KENT

HUCKLES BRIDGE

SOUTH GORLEY

TO FURZE HILL

HARBRIDGE

HARBRIDGE HOUSE

IBSLEY MANOR FARM

TURMER

HARBRIDGE FARM

A 338 TO RINGWOOD

TO MOYLES COURT

AVON VALLEY PATH

KEY
- - - - FOOTPATH
═══ TRACK
━━━ METALLED ROAD
+ CHURCH
□ GENERALISED BUILDING
○ PUBLIC HOUSE
✳ START POINT OF WALK
➤ ROUTE OF WALK

1

NOTE

THIS MAP IS DIAGRAMMATIC ONLY AND IS NOT TO SCALE

IBSLEY

to your right. Within a few hundred yards the ridge path divides. Here you bear right-ahead, downhill, to cross a gravel track and some grass directly beyond. Tnis brings you to a grass-and-gravel track preceding a stile and a fenced path leading downhill to another stile. Beyond this the fenced path continues between paddocks to a bridge across the Huckle Brook, one of those brown streams that flow from the New Forest's western moorlands into the Avon.

Cross a paddock directly ahead now to a stile preceding a lane which you follow right-handed to South Gorley. Where the lane forks keep left-ahead to join another lane along which you continue left-ahead for a few yards to a driveway on your right, almost immediately after entering which you cross a waymarked public footpath stile close to a bungalow on your left. Now follow a fenced path between gardens to a stile beyond which you skirt the near left-hand corner of a nursery to a stile on your left, at a point where a greenhouse lies to your right. Cross this and head diagonally right-handed across a paddock to the next stile, right-ahead. From this carry on in the same direction to where a stile in the hedge to your left leads out on to an unmetalled lane.

Cross this diagonally and the stile now directly in front of you, preceding two paddocks with an intervening stile, which again you cross diagonally. The next stile, in the far hedge, precedes another unmetalled lane with a further stile directly opposite, beyond which you follow the right-hand edge of an enclosed grassy area along what is still part of the public footpath linking South Gorley and Ibsley. You pass through three successive gates before crossing the next stile, beyond which you cross a paddock diagonally to a stile on its far side. Here you enter a field where you head diagonally left from the hedge on your right, on the same footpath alignment as hitherto, to reach and cross a stile just over halfway along the hedge to your left.

Here you join a section of The Avon Valley Path which has been diverted around gravel workings. Its grassy course, hedged on your right, leads you right-handed, bending left and then right before crossing an access route between gravel extraction areas on both sides of the path. Unspoilt rurality promptly returns when you put all this behind you as you continue along the footpath, which follows the left-hand edge of a field to where two adjoining stiles on your left face different directions. Cross the left-hand one to follow the right-hand edge of a field for about 100 yards to a stile in the hedge to your right.

Cross this and the field beyond to a stile in the hedgerow on its far side, after crossing which your footpath follows the left-hand edge of a well-stocked garden. Leaving this by another stile, you follow the left-hand edge of a paddock to what is positively the final stile on this route. You then cross a grassy area to join a road which you follow right-handed, passing Ibsley's old Church of St. Martin — now an art gallery — on your right as you re-emerge on to A338. A few yards along this, to your right, is The Old Beams and the end of your walk.

Avon Valley Paths
near Fordingbridge

WALK 14
At least 4 hours
6 ½ miles
Walk begins page 85

Background to the Walk

Pick any part of it you choose, and the Avon Valley has delights enough to lure any country lover. Now that The Avon Valley Path from Salisbury to Christchurch is available, walkers can enjoy this riverine region in a way not previously possible. You will encounter the long-distance route, with its bridge logo on waymarking signs at appropriate places, at several points on this circular walk, which steers clear of metalled roads for all but a small fraction of its length.

Your starting point, Lower Burgate, is a hamlet just on the Salisbury side of Fordingbridge, with a westerly loop of the Avon sweeping right past it. Burgate House, farther south, in its own grounds adjoining a particularly scenic stretch of the river, is national headquarters of the Game Conservancy, a body devoted to propagating research into the conservation and management of pheasants, partridges, grouse and other game species. Fryern Court, another notable local residence, was the home of artist Augustus John.

Burgate itself, or at any rate Lower Burgate — Upper Burgate is a few hundred yards up the road — has some attractive timber-framed houses. The Tudor Rose and The Hour Glass, nearby, occupy premises which are outstanding examples of the kind. With the noise-polluted present day right on their doorstep, these preserve more than a hint of tranquil times when wheeled traffic on what is now the busy A338 crunched its leisurely way over gravel and was dependent entirely on horsepower.

Burgate, as a placename, has an ancient ring to it.

Maps
Landranger 1:50,000
Sheets 184 and 195
1:25,000
Outdoor Leisure 22, New Forest
Map Reference of Start/Finish
SU153162

How to get there
The walk starts at Lower Burgate, on the Salisbury-Ringwood road just north of Fordingbridge. From Southampton follow A3024, M271 and westbound M27 to Cadnam, B3079 to Brook and B3078 to Fordingbridge bypass, which you follow in the Salisbury direction for under a mile to Lower Burgate, where The Tudor Rose is on your left. Leave Bournemouth via Wessex Way to follow A338 to Ringwood, approaching which you briefly join A31 before filtering left to resume A338, which you follow north around Fordingbridge to Lower Burgate. Wilts & Dorset buses on service X7 from Southampton to Salisbury connect there with those on service X3 between Salisbury, Bournemouth and Poole. Alternatively, Solent Blue Line/Wilts & Dorset services X1, X2 and X5 from Southampton connect with Wilts & Dorset service X3 at Ringwood, stopping at Fordingbridge.

Pub facilities
The Tudor Rose
Lower Burgate
This eyecatching assemblage of thatch, ancient beams and whitewashed walls half-smothered in wisteria is said to date in part from the 14th century and to include an original fireplace. In recent times it has been considerably extended, so harmoniously in character with what was there before that you might never notice the difference. It has been a pub only since around 1970, prior to which it was a French restaurant. Owned by Greenalls and under the same successful management since 1990, it is run as a traditional pub in all respects. Opening times are 1100-1500 and 1800-2300 daily throughout the year. Guest beers are a particular feature, brews being changed at regular intervals but usually including Wadworth 6X, Ringwood Best and Ringwood Forty-Niner. Food may be ordered between 1200-1430 and 1800-2130. The pub has recently undergone refurbishment which includes a completely new decor. The opportunity was taken to introduce an exciting new menu. Comprehensive in character and regularly available, this offers dishes carefully chosen to appeal to the discerning clientele for whom this pub takes pride in catering. The Tudor Rose has built up a reputation for providing the very best of restaurant food and service in an authentic pub atmosphere and this remains the hallmark of their policy for the future. Children are admitted except to the bar area and the menu includes special dishes for children as well as for vegetarians. Walkers may leave their cars in the large pub car park if they are also using the pub. The pub is said to be

The Tudor Rose, Lower Burgate

'Burh', we are reminded, was Old English for 'fortified place'. 'Gate' was apt to mean 'goat', so was there a fortified place here where goats were kept? The combination sounds unlikely, so perhaps 'gate' meant 'gate' after all, with the hamlet being located at the gate of a fortified place. What fortified place, though? A mile away, across the river, is an ancient earthwork called Frankenbury, but surely that is a mite too distant — and indeed on the wrong side of the river.

On this walk you pass through Stuckton, whose name perhaps derives from 'Stockton' meaning 'farmstead at an adjoining hamlet' according to Mills's *Dictionary of English Place-Names*. The same authority suggests that Bickton, also on our route, perhaps means 'farmstead of a man called Bica'. Fordingbridge is less mysterious. There has apparently been a bridge across the Avon there since Saxon times, though the Romans, who came earlier, made do with a ford without a bridge. The seven-arched bridge of today was rebuilt and widened in 1841 to follow the style of its mediaeval original, on which at one time a watchman was stationed to keep an eye on all who passed and make sure the King's game or other property was not being spirited away from the New Forest.

Fordingbridge today is a compact and pleasant

little town bracketing the junction of the old A338 with the road to Cranborne and Wimborne. The Church of St Mary, at its south-western end, has been largely rebuilt more than once, the predominating style being Early English with additional influences from the Decorated and Perpendicular periods. A delightful feature of our own time is the floral carpet made by parishioners towards the end of summer *haunted by the ghost of a Cavalier, who makes his presence known by knocking courteously on a door and then slamming it, a habit so disconcerting that nearly all the interior doors have been removed. To reserve a table telephone 01425 652227.* every second year and laid along the full length of the central aisle. When we looked in while doing this walk a carpet of flowers from local gardens had just been completed and put in place — a superb work of art by any standards and a highly creditable achievement by the team of ladies concerned.

As is the case with Walk 13, some of the footpaths followed on this walk are liable to be flooded in winter, when the River Avon regularly overflows and inundates much of the valley.

Walk 14

Distance: *Allow four hours for this six-and-a-half mile walk.*
Take care as you cross the extremely busy A338 from The Tudor Rose to follow the main road south for a few yards before turning left opposite a thatched and timber-fronted cottage to follow a concreted farm road. This leads to Burgate Manor Farm. The lovely old farmhouse lies in its garden to your left as you approach the farm buildings, just beyond which you fork left where the Avon Valley Path sign at that point indicates. By what is almost certainly the only suspension footbridge in the county, the path you follow crosses the main arm of the Avon — a very substantial body of water by Wessex standards.

'Please bolt the gate' says a notice just ahead of you here on the structure in question. Beyond the gate a raised footpath leads ahead across a typical valley pasture to where a twist in the path precedes a fenced footway, This crosses various concrete-bridged sidestreams of the Avon: 'runners' as these were called by the old-time 'drowners' whose job it was to adjust the sluices controlling their flow. This enabled selected pastures to be flooded in early spring, thereby becoming in the true sense watermeadows where an extra early flush of grass could thus be encouraged.

A gate with a stile alongside it precedes a grass-and-gravel lane, flanked at first by a sidestream to your right, then hedged on both sides as it rises gently away from the river towards Folds Farm. This was the home of the late Oliver Cutts, a millionaire market trader and well-known local personality who began life as a Londoner and later divided his time between running a modest market stall at Salisbury and looking after a smart hotel he owned in the New Forest, where he liked to be known as 'the Master of Rhinefield'. With the black bowler hat and pinstripe suit he wore on all occasions, he was an unforgettable character.

As you approach Folds Farm, ignore the first footpath-signposted track diverging right and carry on past farm buildings to a junction of gravel lanes where another footpath sign points your way right-handed. Accessible to walkers but otherwise private, the uphill gravelled way you follow gives leftward views across a vale where the farmhouse

The footbridge across the River Avon

snuggles in one corner while New Forest woodlands rise beyond. The byway's gradient fairly soon eases, and where woodland appears ahead cross a stile on your right where a yellow waymarking arrow points out the direction now to be followed.

Heading diagonally left from the stile, you follow a fairly well-defined path across what we found as a weedy pasture, descending to a robust wooden stile on the edge of woodland, where we sheltered from a shower and enjoyed our lunchtime picnic. Crossing the stile, your path dips slightly and then climbs leftward to skirt the rim of the prehistoric earthwork called Frankenbury. Perched as this is on the edge of high ground directly above the Avon Valley, it clearly gave the far-reaching views so important to pre-Roman Britons in detecting the approach of hostile intruders.

With the earthwork to your left and a fairly steep beech-clad slope descending to your right, your well-used path curves gently left. With Frankenbury soon behind you, farmland appears to your left and you join a gravel path leading on ahead to a road which you follow through the extensive Sandy Balls Country Holiday Centre. Caravans, tents, chalets and a variety of facilities for the many vacationers who come here succeed each other as you follow the main arterial road of the complex, joined in its turn by various other roads and environed throughout by trees.

Within yards of the main entrance take a right-turning holiday-centre road which, like the road you have been following to this point, is also a public footpath. Metalled at first, the road becomes gravelled as it leads on past residential bungalows to the end of the holiday centre. An arrowed path leads on ahead downhill close to the leftward edge of the wood called Sandy Balls. As you descend steeply to a stile preceding a meadow a superb view across the Avon Valley, directly ahead, presents itself. Cross the stile, and the meadow, to a

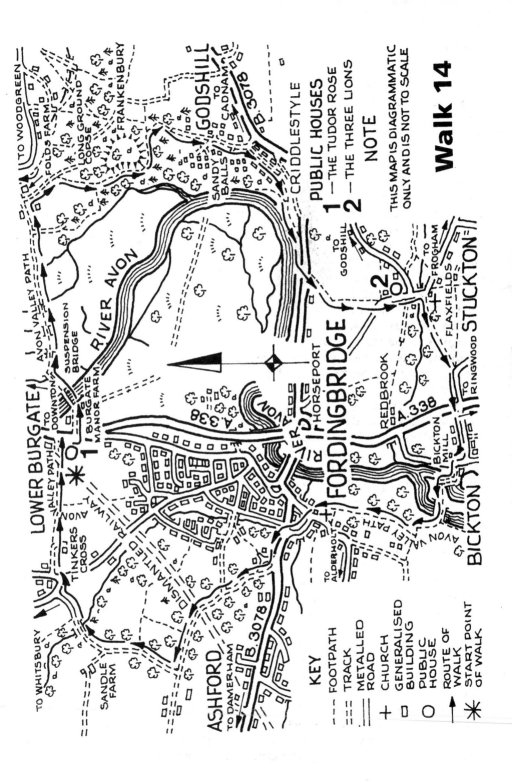

KEY

--- FOOTPATH

=== TRACK

=== METALLED ROAD

+ CHURCH

☐ GENERALISED BUILDING

○ PUBLIC HOUSE

→ ROUTE OF WALK

✳ START POINT OF WALK

PUBLIC HOUSES
1 — THE TUDOR ROSE
2 — THE THREE LIONS

NOTE
THIS MAP IS DIAGRAMMATIC ONLY AND IS NOT TO SCALE

Walk 14

Bickton Mill

kissing-gate leading out on to the Cadnam-Fordingbridge road at Criddlestyle.

Follow the road right-handed, down-hill, to a stile on your left with a footpath sign alongside it. Cross the stile and head diagonally right across the meadow you now enter, keeping a little way to the left of an isolated oak tree in the meadow itself to reach and cross a double stile with an intervening metal footbridge over a stream, just over halfway along the fence on the meadow's far side. After crossing the double stile head diagonally right across the next pasture to another double stile halfway along the hedge on this pasture's right-hand side. Having crossed this, follow the left-hand edge of the pasture beyond to the next stile, beyond which your path is fenced on both sides, with a hedge as well on your left. A stile at the end of this leads out on to a lane which you follow left-ahead through Stuckton, passing The Three Lions restaurant on your left.

Carry on through Stuckton, one of a series of mini-villages flanking the New Forest's western borderland and stretching south to Ringwood and beyond. After crossing a stream called Ditchend Brook turn right by a telephone kiosk to follow a streamside track and path, with Stuckton's Evangelical Church and a graveyard to your left. Beyond a decayed wicket-gate a hedged path leads away from the stream to your right and brings you soon to a stile preceding a meadow, the right-hand edge of which you follow for about 50 yards before bearing half-left and heading towards a double stile two-thirds of the way along the far hedge. Cross this and head diagonally across the pasture beyond to its far corner, where a stile serving your own path and another path which converges from your left precedes a lane which you follow right-handed.

Not many yards ahead you cross A338 and continue along another lane into Bickton, a little Avon Valley village just far enough from the main road to preserve a measure of old-time peace and with more than a sprinkling of thatch among its dwellings. Some of the house names tell their own story: The Old Malt House, for one, and Forge Cottage for another — the village blacksmith's hammer is silent now and has been for many a year. The White House, on your left, is not one of Bickton's older dwellings — not as old, at any rate, as The Old White House directly opposite, as its name makes a point of emphasising.

When you reach a T-junction turn right, then within a matter of yards you pass Bickton Mill, now transformed into residential accommodation. The old mill-race is spanned by a road bridge and a separate footpath bridge. These precede a right-turning track that bridges the Avon's main arm, which is substantial enough, we noted, to be favoured by a bird which likes fairly sizeable sheets of water, the great crested grebe. Swans, coots and moorhens are also in evidence hereabouts.

When you soon reach private ground surrounded by high fencing turn left to follow a fenced footpath, plainly signposted. After bridging various Avon sidestreams, your path follows the left-hand edge of a pasture and joins the Avon Valley Path before reaching and following for a few yards the right-hand edge of another pasture. From this the route of your well-trodden path soon angles left across the pasture, from the far side of which it is fenced and punctuated, by frequent kissing-gates for the rest of the way to Fordingbridge. Here you emerge by St Mary's Church, where the floral carpet laid every other year had just been completed and put into position along the central aisle when we called. On each occasion the carpet has a theme appropriate to the year.

Pass right-handed of the church to leave the churchyard by its main entrance. Follow the road ahead for a short distance, then turn left along quiet West Street to join and follow left-handed Station Road. Since the Salisbury to West Moors railway was closed in the mid-'60s, only the local police station remains to make sense of the road name. Just past this outpost of law and order turn right to follow Marl Lane, which at first is scarcely more than a footpath. It widens into an unmetalled road skirting left of housing development and then heading north-west away from the town, with a country house used nowadays as a school set amid parkland to your left.

Two hundred yards or so after crossing an old railway arch turn right at a junction of gravel lanes bordered by lime trees and head north. You soon pass Sandle Farm with its pond in the foreground on your left before crossing tree-shaded Sweatfords Water. An unsuspected heron took wing when I glanced over the parapet of the bridge which spans this brook. From the point just a little way farther on where you pass a power transformer the lane becomes metalled and leads uphill to Tinkers Cross. Here you turn right at a T-junction.

At a further lane junction just ahead turn left, then almost immediately turn right to follow a hedged gravel lane with a footpath sign at the start of it. Where the second of two private driveways soon bears right the gravel ends. Carry on ahead along a hedged path which changes back into an unmetalled road as you approach Lower Burgate. When you reach the main road turn right; The Tudor Rose is just ahead.

Downland Ways near Whitsbury

WALK 15
At least 3 hours
5 ½ miles
Walk begins page 93

Background to the Walk

Whitsbury is one of those tucked-away villages which look to having been well and truly sheltered from the world's tempests almost since the beginning of time. Closer inspection, however, reveals it as the location of a substantial fortified earthwork dating from the pre-Roman period and strongly suggestive of unchronicled conflicts well before the dawn of history. It may well have been from Whitsbury Castle that native Britons engaged invading Saxons in battle at nearby Charford in an unavailing effort to hold them on the line of the Avon. Either way, the Iron Age stronghold formed one of a chain of such defences parallel with the river's course form Old Sarum southward and therefore probably delineating some sort of tribal frontier where warfare was apt to flare up at intervals.

As if to crown and confirm all this, placename pundits tell us that the name Whitsbury derives from the 12th century 'Wiccheberia', meaning 'fortified place where wych-elms grow'. This in turn derives from 'Witeberge', which rated a mention in Domesday. The village became monastic property linked with the priory at Breamore up to the time of the Dissolution. A later owner was the Earl of Shaftesbury. At one time an annual hog fair was held here. This ceased in 1825, but the village remained mainly agricultural, with most of its menfolk being employed on farms until well within living memory.

There has been a church at Whitsbury since at least the 13th century. In 1877 the then incumbent, a member of the Purvis family who were prominent in

Maps
Landranger 1:50,000
Sheet 184
1:25,000
Outdoor Leisure 22, New Forest and Explorer 130, Salisbury and Stonehenge
Map Reference of Start/Finish
SU128188

How to get there
Whitsbury lies 3 miles north-west of the Avon Valley town of Fordingbridge. From Southampton head west along A3024, M271 and M27 to Cadnam, then follow B3079 to Brook and B3078 from there to Fordingbridge, passing under Fordingbridge bypass to follow the old main road right-handed immediately east of the town centre, directly beyond which you turn left to follow the signposted road to Whitsbury. From Bournemouth follow Wessex Way and A338 to Ringwood, briefly joining A31 there before filtering left to resume A338, which you follow north to Fordingbridge, turning off it to follow the old main road skirting Fordingbridge town centre, just beyond which you turn left to follow the signposted route to Whitsbury. Buses to and from Whitsbury, Salisbury and Fordingbridge are for the convenience of shoppers and operate on certain days only at times unsuitable for walkers reliant on buses, who are advised to start the walk at

The Cartwheel, Whitsbury

local life throughout most of the 19th century, had the church extensively restored, so that what we see today is a simple but striking brick-built structure with a tall, slim western tower and a barrel-vaulted nave. Further restorative work was undertaken in 1963. The path leading up to it from the village is so steep that old-time undertakers' men sometimes stumbled with their burdens while carrying coffins for burial services. This was remedied by the construction of a longer but much less steeply graded route to the hilltop church.

Between the church and Glebe House, which was formerly the rectory and is Whitsbury's only listed building, remains of a Roman building complete with hypocaust (or under floor heating system) have been found. Roman coins and other relics have also come to light at Whitsbury Castle, providing evidence of its use in some form subsequent to the Iron Age.

The original Whitsbury Manor House was demolished in 1826. The house so-called today is a focal point of Whitsbury Manor Stud. Horses bred and trained here include some of the most famous names in racing, Desert Orchid being among them. Racing is the life-blood of the community today. Grazing paddocks for horses surround the village, and the gallops for which the surrounding downland is so well suited are much in evidence on this walk.

Breamore, alighting by the village post office. Opposite the Bat & Ball pub follow a road which heads west to a fork. Bear left here and at the next T-junction turn right, then almost immediately turn left to join the route as described at that point. Bus access from Southampton is via Wilts & Dorset service X7 to Salisbury or Solent Blue Line/Wilts & Dorset service X1, X2 or X5 to Ringwood, changing at either of these places to Wilts & Dorset service X3 between Poole, Bournemouth and Salisbury, which passes through Breamore.

Pub facilities
The Cartwheel, Whitsbury.
An eyecatching blend of period beams and brickwork, this free house occupies premises which until about 1970 also included the village shop. At one time a wheelwright was based here and the wheel of a cart is embodied in a partition between two sections of the bar which, with the restaurant, now occupies almost the whole of the building's ground floor. Pub decor includes skilfully executed drawings of dogs of various breeds and pictures of horses as a reminder of the links of the village with racing. A good selection of real ales includes Ringwood Forty-Niner, Ringwood True Glory, Fuller's London Pride and Adnam's Broadside. Also on draught are Murphy's Irish stout, Guinness, seven draught lagers and three ciders. A menu common to bar and restaurant offers such specials as chicken curry with rice, poppadums and accompaniments, 6oz sirloin steak garni, prawn and mushroom pasta parmagiana and 12 inch deep pan pizza with onion, tomato, mushroom and mozzarella topping. Meat dishes range from steak and

kidney pie, smoked gammon steak, roast chicken quarter and 8oz rump steak to Continental special pizza, chilli con carne, lasagne verdi and ham and mushroom pasta. Among fish dishes you can take your choice from breaded scampi, rainbow trout, swordfish steak, grilled whole plaice, seafood salad, breaded cod fillet or tuna and pineapple pizza. A good range of starters, desserts and vegetarian dishes are also available. There is a garden and children's play area. Children may eat in the pub restaurant but are not permitted in the bar area. An open fire warms the bar in winter. Walkers using the pub may leave their cars in the pub car park but are advised to arrive early to find space on Sundays especially. Pub opening hours are 1100-1430 (until 1500 on Saturdays) and 1800-2300 on weekdays and 1200-1500 and 1900-2230 on Sundays. Food may be ordered between 1200-1400 and 1900-2130 but on Tuesdays is only available at lunchtime. The telephone number is 01725 518362.

For the rest, the countryside round about is a mixture of sloping arable fields broken up by belts and clumps of timber, with larger woodlands stretching south and east towards the Avon Valley.

In many ways the scenery is typical of south Wiltshire. Until 1895, indeed, Whitsbury was in Wiltshire. Its transfer that year to Hampshire is a reminder that alterations to county boundaries in our own time are by no means the first to have changed the shape of the ancient shires of Wessex, something of a culture shock though this is to many who live in the counties concerned.

Breamore, next door, is truly ancient. Its church was built about AD980, a date not forgotten a thousand years later when millenary celebrations included refurbishment of wall paintings from times well before the Dissolution. A striking feature of the building is the extensive use made of flints in its construction. Fully exposed to our view today, in pre-Norman times, experts tell us, they would have been covered over in plaster.

Not all of the church is of quite such great antiquity. The east doorway is typically Norman, and the chancel was largely rebuilt in the 14th century, but the long-and-short quoins of the central tower and the stonework of the south transept are among substantial relics which make this place of worship at Breamore the best-preserved Saxon church in Hampshire. Another feature of special note is the Saxon stone rood above the nave doorway, depicting Christ with the Virgin Mary and St John. This has been badly mutilated, probably under instructions from Bishop Robert Horne of Winchester not many years after the Dissolution.

The pre-Reformation church was associated with Breamore Priory, situated alongside the Avon a little way north of Breamore Mill. The surrounding watermeadows have been maintained as such for centuries, but when the priory was first established as a house of the Austin canons during the reign of Henry I, this flat land may still have retained the character of the broomy moor or marsh which first gave rise to the name of Breamore.

Following the Dissolution in 1536, the manor of Breamore and another manor were given to Henry, Marquess of Exeter, a grandson of Edward IV. He was not to enjoy his good fortune for long. Just two years later Henry VIII, suspecting the marquess as having designs on the throne, had his head cut off. A later owner was William Doddington, Treasurer to Elizabeth I, who in 1583 built that

On the downs near Whitsbury

far-famed specimen of Elizabeth architecture, Breamore House. Backed by extensive hilltop woodland and flanked by beautifully timbered parkland which slopes gently down to the half-mile distant A338 and the Avon Valley, the mansion has been home to many generations of Hulses. It is opened to the public, while another estate attraction is a countryside museum with exhibits highlighing various aspects of rural life as lived in the past.

At one time clustered about the church, which lies just in front of Breamore House, the present-day village of Breamore largely dates from the 17th century and has its centre on the main road. Its mellow cottages of warm brick with their characteristic leadlight windows have that unity of style which confirms common origin and ownership as homes for those whose livelihoods were linked with the local 'big house' and with the estate of which Breamore continues to form part. Let no one hear you call it 'Bree-moor'. 'Bremmer' is how the locals pronounce it, and so, apparently, have their forebears ever since the days of the Saxons.

Between Whitsbury and Breamore are two other notable antiquities. Giant's Grave, on Breamore Down, is a prehistoric long barrow 60 yds in length and 28 yds wide at its wider end. It has been damaged by cultivation. Better preserved is the Mizmaze, hidden away in a hilltop yew grove and protected from casual wear and tear by a fence and a cautionary notice requesting visitors just to look but not to walk on its fragile turf. The notice describes it as prehistoric. Its significance is unknown and it is scheduled now as a nationally important site as recognised by the Ancient Monuments and Archaeological Areas Act of 1979. You will see it on this walk along with a wealth of delightful scenery.

Walk 15

Distance: *Allow three hours for this five-and-a-half mile walk.*
Leave The Cartwheel pub at Whitsbury behind you on your left as you head south-east along the village road for a few yards before turning left to follow a fenced path steeply uphill to a latched gate. Cross the rising pasture beyond,

making a bee-line for the church at the top of the hill ahead of you. A second latched gate leads into the churchyard. The church, with its latticed nave windows and its plain, whitewashed interior projecting an image of pleasing simplicity, is normally open to visitors. We found it filled with flowers in readiness for a village wedding.

From outside the nave door follow a churchyard path right-handed around the rear of the building and out through a gate to follow left-handed a grass-centred gravel track. Hedged on your left and flanked by racehorse paddocks on your right, this fairly soon joins a metalled driveway which you follow ahead, downhill, disregarding turnings left and right to re-emerge on to the village road. Follow this right-handed for a few yards, then turn right through a gate alongside which a footpath sign points the way past the buildings of Whitsbury Manor Stud. Outbuildings include thatched barns with beams both vertically and diagonally — fine-looking structures indeed these are.

At the end of the buildings turn right to skirt the stud and follow a view-commanding track of grass and chalk with a fence on your left and Whitsbury Castle's triple ramparts mantled in woodland to your right. Whitsbury Manor Farm is reached by a side-turning to your left, but you continue ahead on a scenic descent into a vale beyond which cereal-growing downland is patterned with strips and tufts of timber.

At the valley bottom cross a broad, grassy drove and a stile on the other side of it to follow a footpath along the right-hand edge of arable land on rising ground with a hedgerow to your right. You soon skirt right-handed of the southern end of a small wood of yews and beeches, then follow a track straight on through this wood to emerge on its far side. Carry on ahead uphill along the right-hand edge of a field, with a hedge to your right.

This brings you to a stile beyond which your path joins a green lane at the southern extremity of a conifer plantation, with the Avon Valley in view away to your left as you follow the green lane right-handed. Soon emerging on to a patch of open downland, you follow a grass track which here bears right to climb to the edge of the grove of yews which masks the Mizmaze. Carry on along the woodland margin to a junction of tracks where you turn right to pass a white notice-board marking the entry point for the path leading through the yew grove to the Mizmaze. This occupies a circular site with alternating shallow chalk trenches and turfy pathways forming a pattern which, from the outside, does not look unduly difficult to fathom and work out how to reach the centre. As already mentioned, you are asked not to attempt this except as a mental exercise.

Walk out through the yews the way you came in and then bear right to follow a downhill path to rejoin and follow right-handed the green lane you left after briefly following it from the southern end of the conifer plantation. As you now continue along it, trees and shrubs flank your way uphill to a fork of tracks where a green lane signposted as a permissive path leads straight ahead but

Walk 15

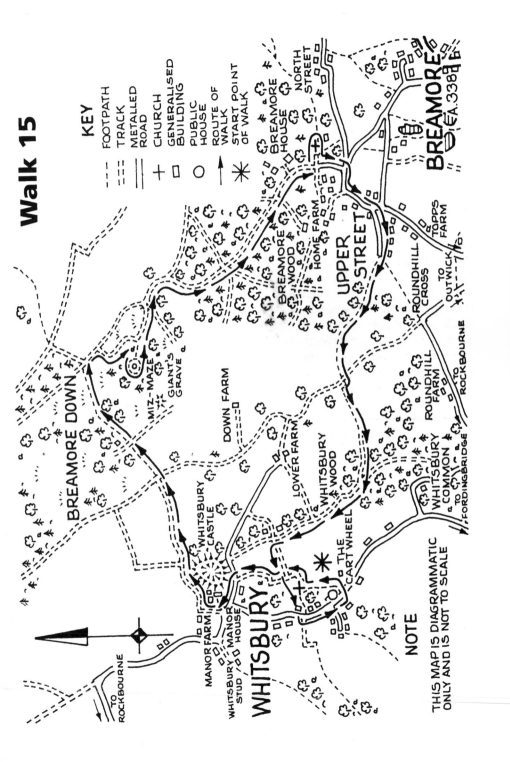

where you bear right. The well-used track you now follow winds through the old oaks and beeches of Breamore Wood, in which the numerous side-turnings are marked 'private' and therefore need cause no confusion.

A descent of several hundred yards precedes the point where you leave the wood to skirt an expanse of parkland and pass within yards of Breamore House before continuing downhill along what is now a metalled drive to where a side turning to your left leads to the Saxon church at Breamore. Spare time for at least a peep at this before returning to the main driveway and continuing downhill. Unless the countryside museum and adjacent tearooms are on your personal itinerary, ignore the right-hand turning to these and carry on to the next road crossing.

Turn right here to follow a lane from which two driveways bear right at a bend from which your lane turns left. Following the public road, you head past the houses of Upper Street, an outlying part of Breamore proper. Eyecatching period dwellings are half-screened by mellow old walls as you approach the next lane turning. Here you turn right to follow what soon becomes a cottage-flanked cul-de-sac. Where dwellings soon end, so too does the metalled road, and you continue along a tree-lined track. Where the track itself soon forks left, keep straight on along what is now a mere path hemmed in by burgeoning vegetation.

This ends at a stile, which you cross to follow a footpath downhill along the left-hand edge of farmland, with a hedge and an ancient hollow lane, now largely weed-filled, just to your left. At a valley bottom, which you soon reach, you pass through a gate to join an unmetalled farm road, which you follow right-handed for a few yards before turning left through a pedestrian gate to follow a rising footpath along the right-hand edge of arable farmland, with a wood on the high ground ahead. Your footpath carries on into this wood, where diverging rides and tracks are clearly marked 'private'.

Fairly soon reaching the wood's far side, carry on along the edge of it for several hundred yards, with horse paddocks to your left. When you draw parallel with a semi-bungalow on your right, turn left to follow a railed path between paddocks. This leads to a T-junction of fenced paths where you turn left for Whitsbury church, heading right-handed through the churchyard to follow another fenced path which winds steeply downhill to reach the village road. Follow this left-handed to retrieve your car from the pub car park.

Wiltshire Chalk near Charlton All Saints

WALK 16
At least 3 hours
6 ½ miles
Walk begins page 99

Background to the Walk

Charlton, experts remind us, is one of England's commoner placenames, there being no fewer than three in Wiltshire alone. With one or two exceptions, its first syllable derives from the Old English 'ceorl', meaning 'freeman', 'peasant' or 'person of low birth' — whence the modern word 'churl', which has come to signify a boorish, ill-bred, cross-grained or niggardly person! The plural is 'ceorla', and 'tun' means 'farmstead' so the name Charlton may be interpreted as 'farmstead of the freemen or peasants'.

Charlton All Saints is the full name of this quiet mini-village on the banks of the River Avon, reached by lanes which lead nowhere else but linked by footpaths with Bodenham, Downton and elsewhere in the vicinity. It lies on The Avon Valley Path, a walking route which follows the river valley south from Salisbury, and is overlooked from both east and west by the rolling south Wiltshire chalkland, much of which was at one time common grazing land for sheep. There are still some sheep on these downs but the growing of cereals is now the main agricultural activity. The New Forest is not far away — a mere three miles in a south-easterly direction — and can be clearly seen from high ground to the west in the course of this walk.

Prominent on this high ground, crowning Clearbury Down, less than two miles away, is Clearbury Ring, where mantling woodland hides the earthworks of a substantial Iron Age hill fort. You will skirt this on the walk and, looking east, you will see peeping out from the trees beyond the Avon Trafalgar

Maps
Landranger 1:50,000
Sheet 184
1:25,000
Explorer 130, Salisbury and Stonehenge
Map Reference of Start/Finish
SU169240

How to get there
The Stag at Charlton lies on the east side of A338, the Salisbury-Ringwood road, about 4 miles south-east of Salisbury and 1½ miles north of Downton, which can be reached from Southampton via A3024, M271, westbound M27 to Cadnam, then via B3079 to Brook, B3078 to Bramshaw Telegraph and then B3080 via Redlynch, continuing through Downton itself to join and follow right-handed A338. From Bournemouth follow Wessex Way and A338 to its junction with A31 at Ringwood, where you resume A338 and follow it north, skirting Fordingbridge and Downton en route to your starting-point at The Stag. Wilts & Dorset buses on service X7 from Southampton and on Solent Blue Line/Wilts & Dorset services X1, X2 and X5 connect at Salisbury and Ringwood respectively with Wilts & Dorset service X3 between Poole, Bournemouth and Salisbury.

Pub Facilities
The Stag, Charlton
This freehouse pub is an ideal stopping-off point for travellers on the Avon Valley main road between Salisbury, Ringwood and Bournemouth. Originally an estate house built about 200 years ago, it has a south-facing, sunny aspect and is a nice, bright pub attracting a clientele from many miles around as well as a busy passing trade. Popular brews include Ringwood and Courage beers, selected guest ales, draught Guinness, Foster's and McEwen's lagers and dry Blackthorn cider. This is pre-eminently a food pub catering for families and children, for whom there is a trampoline and a climbing frame in the garden. The lunch menu offers items such as Cornish pastie, half a roast chicken, home-made shepherd's pie and steak and kidney pie, gammon steak with egg or pineapple, 8oz sirloin steak garni, chicken curry and southern fried chicken, not forgetting three vegetarian dishes, five fish dishes and a choice of four ploughman's. Salads, sandwiches, sweets, ice cream and a special children's menu are also available. Specials when we called included chicken cordon bleu (filled with ham and cheese) and home-made tuna quiche, plus lemon sorbet, hot chocolate fudge cake and lemon tart with ice cream. Food may be ordered at any time during opening hours, which are 1100-1500 and 1800-2300 on weekdays and 1200-1500 and 1900-2230 on Sundays. Walkers using the pub are welcome to use the large pub car park. The telephone number is 01722 329708.

The Stag, Charlton All Saints

House, built as Standlynch House in 1733 and renamed after the famous battle when presented by the nation to Nelson's heirs, who lived here until the present century.

Most of the land hereabouts forms part of the Earl of Radnor's Longford Castle estate. Longford Castle itself lies in a 250-acre park alongside the Avon and is a triangular house of 16th century origin. It was built by Sir Thomas Gorges, who ran out of money before it was finished. The day was saved when one of the ships of the Spanish Armada ran aground on coastal property belonging to Sir Thomas. His wife, a lady-in-waiting to Queen Elizabeth I, petitioned the monarch to allow her husband to take possession of the wreck. This turned out to be laden with treasure which amply restored Sir Thomas's fortune.

This walk covers two entirely different types of country. All but the final two miles explores the broad tract of virtually uninhabited downland stretching west from A338 just north of Downton to meet A354, the Salisbury-Blandford road, south of Coombe Bissett. This hilly land of wide open spaces is not only largely unpeopled but almost devoid of metalled roads, which makes it a region of rare serenity, with only the rumble of a tractor or two or the dust-disturbing passage of some farmer's or gamekeeper's Land-Rover to intrude on the rural quiet. Here, indeed, is a land where you can truly walk in peace, at one with nature, or such part of it as agricultural man has harmonised with his own interests: a not ungenerous portion, you are likely to agree. Leaving the high ground for the valley, you traverse field paths around Charlton, a country community all the more special for being 'on the road to

In the distance is tree-crowned Clearbury Ring

nowhere' and therefore having to be sought out by those from outside who would like to know more about it.

Walk 16

Distance: *Allow 3 hours for this walk of about six-and-a-half miles.*
Almost opposite the turning for Charlton next to The Stag you follow a hedged metalled lane heading west towards the downs on that side of A338. Within a few hundred yards roadmetal ends where the made-up road turns right at the entrance to Charlton Manor Farm, and you will not see tarmac again until towards the end of the walk when you rejoin and cross the Avon Valley highway a mile farther north. Continue along a gravel byway, rising gently and curving left-handed as you follow a dry valley bottom, with a wooded bank to your left.

Leaving the valley, the byway soon becomes grassy rather than gravelled as you continue a steady ascent to where Warren Plantation lies to your left. All the way towards this isolated hillside wood the view to your right is dominated by Clearbury Ring with its topnotch of trees, here less than a mile distant. Your grass track, as it now is, winds on and up past cattle-grazed slopes and corn-growing expanses to skirt the next pocket-handkerchief woodland, Charlton Furze, on your right-hand side.

These scattered boscages do much to enhance the scenic charm of the chalkland, breaking up, as they do, the pattern of otherwise endless undulations of mainly cereal-growing country: refreshingly spacious and uncluttered by extraneous visual elements but all the better for a modest admixture, as here, of timbered verdure. Carry on to the end of Charlton Furze, where you emerge through a gateway to join a gravel road at the most distant point of this walk from where you started, now almost three miles below and behind you. Here, on these broad and breezy uplands, we used a wayside horse-jumping trestle as a seat for our picnic lunch while enjoying the peace of our surroundings. We also relished the easterly view across the valley from which we had climbed, where tree-fringed fields beyond the Avon mingled with woods away to the south, with farmland and forest coming together on the Fordingbridge side of Downton.

Having joined the gravel road, follow its wide, straight course right-handed, north-east, with the beeches and conifers of Charlton Furze still to your right. To your rear the view is bounded by the distant green ridge of Martin Down, on the Hampshire-Dorset border, as you climb gently for half-a-mile before descending past a small wood on your left to a right-hand gate with a bridleway sign. Pass through this gateway to follow a grass track, hedged to your left but unfenced on your right, which continues north-east with Clearbury Ring now directly in front of you, presenting an ever more dramatic view beyond trees in a valley ahead as you draw closer.

After crossing a stile next to a wooden gate, flanked in its turn by a metal gate, you disregard a right-forking track and keep to the main one, leading left-ahead downhill past a belt of scrub, with a hedge to your left. You then skirt left of what we found as a downland pasture bespangled with flowers and dancing with butterflies of many hues on a bright, warm day in summer. Your track now rises to the edge of Clearbury Ring, which it follows right-handed to a gate and stile at the south-east end of the wooded earthwork. From here we crossed the outer ditch to mount and circumnavigate the rim of the hill fort itself, now mantled in a luxuriant growth of beech, ash and sycamore, which also covers the central area enclosed within the earthwork.

From the gate and stile last mentioned, carry on along the grass track around the outer edge of Clearbury Ring to a point directly opposite where you reached its periphery. Here your track turns away from it to head for the Avon Valley, now spread before you with Pepperbox Hill in view in the background, while beyond a left-hand hedge the spire of Salisbury Cathedral looms in the middle-distance. A quarter-of-a-mile downhill the well-defined track angles slightly right. You follow a lesser track left-handed to the near side of a gate, where you turn right to follow the left-hand edge of an arable field, with a hedge to your left.

After descending for half-a-mile you join and follow ahead part of The Avon Valley Path, a long distance walking route from Salisbury opened in 1992 as a means of exploring the river valley while avoiding roads as far as possible. This leads on down to a gateway where you cross A338. After crossing two stiles on the main road's far side you head diagonally right across a pasture towards a gate at its far corner, through which you pass to join and follow right-handed a dark and narrow tree-lined lane.

This passes Matrimony Farm about a quarter-of-a-mile before bending right,

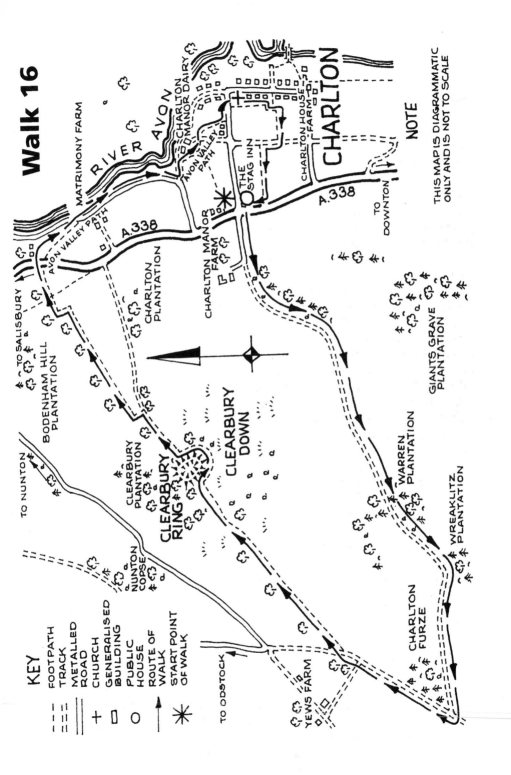

All Saints Church, Charlton

at which point you cross a stile left-ahead of you to follow a fenced footpath, hedged on your right, with a concrete farm road to your left. Where the fenced path ends cross a stile and head diagonally across the meadow beyond to a further stile at its far corner. Cross this to follow another fenced path, hedged on your left this time, to the next stile, after crossing which you follow a muddy lane for a few yards to where this bends right. Go through a kissing-gate ahead to continue along the signposted Avon Valley Path. This heads diagonally away from the right-hand edge of the field beyond to reach a stile to the left of some cottages.

Cross the stile to follow the lane beyond left-handed to where a gate on your right precedes a path across Charlton churchyard. The modest, brick-built structure of bell-turreted All Saints Church, erected in 1851, lies to your left here and the door was locked when we passed. Pass through a further gate to follow a fenced path ahead, with Charlton's cottages to your left. When you come to a T-junction of footpaths cross a stile on your right to follow the left-hand edge of a pasture to a further stile preceding a hedged, muddy lane. Follow this lane right-handed to a somewhat rickety stile a few yards along on your left, which you cross to follow the left-hand edge of a meadow to another stile leading out on to A338. A bordering paved footpath leads right-handed for the few remaining yards to where you started. I hope you have planned your walk to arrive at a time when The Stag will be open.

A Wiltshire Walk from Whaddon

WALK 17
Allow 2 or 3 hours
3 or 5 ½ miles
Walk begins page 104

Background to the Walk

This walk starts under the lee of the chalk which rises east of the Avon Valley, south of Salisbury, to form a ridge extending from Pepperbox Hill along the length of Dean Hill and terminating just inside Hampshire. Whether the full circuit or the shorter version is opted for, the combination of hill and vale, with the extensive views that go with this, make the route a highly scenic one.

Whaddon, where the walk begins, was recorded in Domesday Book as 'Waterdene', meaning 'valley where wheat is grown'. Plenty of wheat is still grown in the area, mainly, however, on the chalk, much of the valley land now being pasture. A certain amount of woodland survives from the old Royal Forest of Clarendon, which played an important part in the history of this corner of south-east Wiltshire. As a plaque in The Three Crowns pub reminds us, between the reign of Henry I and that of Richard III, Clarendon Palace, some three miles to the north, was an important royal residence where kings and their courtiers came to hunt. It also served as a place of confinement when in 1357, following the Battle of Poitiers, defeated King John II of France was brought here as a prisoner by King Edward III of England, who also held captive until his release that year King David II of Scotland — a combination of circumstances preserved in memory by the name of the Whaddon hostelry.

Clarendon Palace today is a ruin which may be visited by appointment with the owners of the Clarendon estate, on which it lies. This is one of two

Maps
Landranger 1:50,000
Sheet 184
1:25,000
Explorer 130, Salisbury and Stonehenge, and 131, Romsey, Andover & Test Valley
Map Reference of Start/Finish
SU197260

How to get there
From Southampton follow A3024, M271, westbound M27 and then A36 into Wiltshire. Nearly a mile beyond Pepperbox Hill fork left-ahead as if for Alderbury and within about 100 yards turn left into the car park of The Three Crowns at Whaddon. Leave Bournemouth via Wessex Way to follow A338, eastbound A31 briefly, then A338 again to Salisbury Ring Road (Churchill Way), from which turn right to follow Southampton-signposted A36. Bear right from this at the first turn-off for Alderbury, through which carry straight on to adjacent Whaddon, where The Three Crowns lies well back from the road on your right after passing Alderbury post office on your left. Wilts & Dorset buses on service X7 pass through Whaddon, connecting at Salisbury with service X3 to and from Poole and Bournemouth.

Pub facilities
The Three Crowns
Facing a section of the old main

road between Southampton and Salisbury which was bypassed decades ago, and looking out to a successor highway which has been bypassed in its turn, this hostelry claims links with a time when crowned heads from three countries were present in the neighbourhood — and may actually have been guests here. Beams, ancient brickwork and a welcoming log fire in the cooler months highlight the character of a pub where traditional hospitality is the order of the day. Morland brews can be sampled here. Their real ales include Old Speckled Hen (a strong beer) and hand drawn Morland Original. Bass, Ruddles Best, Ringwood Bitter, Foster's and Stella Artois lagers as well as Scrumpy Jack cider are also on draught. A generous bar menu includes soup, pate, prawn cocktail, plaice, scampi, mixed grills, chicken Kiev, shredded chicken cooked with mushrooms, ginger and cream with egg noodles (a house speciality), home-made steak and kidney pie, fish of the day in home-made beer batter, toasties, burgers, filled jacket potatoes, salads, sandwiches and four types of ploughman's. Roast beef and Yorkshire pudding with onion gravy and fresh vegetables, preceded by soup, pate or fruit juice and followed by apple pie with cream attract many for Sunday lunch here. Pool and darts may be played in the separate games room and there is a large family garden with many amusements for children including swings, a seesaw, climbing frames and Wendy houses. Children may be brought into the restaurant. Bed and breakfast en suite accommodation with bathroom and shower is an additional facility. Walkers may use the large pub car park or the section of old road facing the pub. Hours are 1100-1500 and

The Three Crowns, Whaddon

large landed properties in Whaddon's immediate neighbourhood, the other being the Longford Castle estate of the Earl of Radnor. Much of the ground covered on this walk is Longford Castle property.

Whaddon and Alderbury are virtually one community. The latter is so much the larger that it dominates its neighbour, the separate identity of which is apt to be overlooked by those who are unfamiliar with the area. Alderbury, too, has become a backwater half-forgotten by the great wide world beyond now that through traffic on the A36 has been diverted around it — much to the satisfaction, no doubt, of local people intent on enjoying a peaceful life unmarred by cars and heavy transport constantly racing past their doors. Also departed is the railway that once branched off at Alderbury to follow the Avon Valley south by way of Downton and Fordingbridge, eventually joining the old Southampton-Dorchester main line at West Moors.

Walk 17

Distance: *Allow 2 hours for the three mile version, 3 hours for the full five-and-a-half mile walk.*

From the south side of The Three Crowns, follow the stub of the old road on that side of the pub in a westerly direction, around a metal gate across it not many yards from the pub. The scrub-bordered remnants of this road precede a metalled footpath which leads out on to the slip road from the A36 into Alderbury. Follow this ahead for a few yards, then, almost opposite Alderbury post office and general stores, turn left to follow a poorly-surfaced side road.

1800-2300 from Mondays to Fridays, 1100-2300 on Saturdays and 1200-2230 on Sundays, and food may be ordered between 1200-1400 and 1900-2100 seven days a week. The telephone number is 01722 710211.

Flanked by dwellings, this bends right at its junction with a farm road, signposted 'Pack Path', which you ignore. Carry on to where the road splits into three and turn sharp left to follow a tree-shaded track-cum-driveway. Where this soon ends a narrow but well-defined public footpath leads ahead at first and then angles right through an area of weedy waste ground where bracken grows tall and dense in summer. The path continues into a meadow through which it veers left before emerging through a gap alongside a stile into a lane which you follow right-handed.

After passing Rectory Farm at Alderbury on your left this lane soon bends right at a point from which you follow a hedged and fenced path straight ahead. This path curves right and then left to reach a stile, after crossing which the well-used footway veers left across a meadow, with trees to your left. Beyond a further stile you cross another meadow, about halfway across which is another stile sometimes used when the pasture is sub-divided by electric fencing for grazing purposes.

At the meadow's far side cross another stile, beyond which your path continues ahead with a fence on your left, being fenced on both sides as it approaches a kissing-gate preceding a hedged grass-and-gravel track, which you follow left-handed. This heads downhill to a metalled road, which you follow left-handed in its turn, with the Avon Valley's level pastures spreading to your right and hedged chalk downland rising beyond.

The tree-capped knoll most prominent as you look across the valley is Clearbury Ring, an Iron Age hill fort that dominates the landscape on that side at almost all stages of the walk from this point onward.

Carry on past farm buildings on your left, ignoring turnings left in their immediate vicinity, and stay on the lightly-used road until it emerges from a shallow wooded cutting not far ahead. This is where you turn left to follow a gated gravel road, with trees to your left and arable farmland to your right as it leads you eastward, rising steadily.

When you reach the far end of the field on your right leave the gravel road and turn right to follow a well-defined field-edge bridleway, with a strip of woodland on your left. Where a hillside wood soon confronts you the bridleway heads left-handed through it, with timbered ground rising to your right. Within yards of the wood end tracks divide, one swinging right, another emerging directly on to farmland and a third bearing left to a horse-jumping trestle which served me well as a seat for a lunchtime picnic.

From here the bridleway emerges through beech trees to follow the left-hand edge of a large tract of arable downland, with Pepperbox Hill on the skyline ahead and a wide sweep of chalk country extending well to your right. Although the Ordnance map still depicts a bridleway branching right from the one you are following to converge

A railway arch once spanned this farm road

with the still plainly visible course of the old Salisbury-West Moors railway, which was closed in the 1960s, no trace of a right-of-way on this route has existed for some years now. The bridleway has been moved a little way east and nowadays flanks the former railway, as official waymarking signs confirm.

If you prefer the three-mile walk, this latter detail is immaterial, for all you have to do is to keep straight on along the field-edge bridleway after leaving the wood. This brings you to a bridge where you cross the former railway before following a gently-rising track along the right-hand edge of the field directly beyond. Within a few hundred yards you then turn left to head back to Whaddon along a grassy track between two arable fields.

Time and energy permitting I very strongly recommend the longer walk, if only for the sake of the views to be enjoyed along parts of it. To follow it, on the near side of the old railway arch turn right to follow a well-used bridle-track alongside the earthworks of the old line. As already indicated, this is the current route of the bridleway which formerly crossed the farmland a little way west. It heads downhill to cross a farm road which was once spanned by a railway arch directly to your left. You then continue ahead, uphill, and then gently down to a gate through which you enter the next field to follow its leftward edge straight on.

At the end of this field the well-defined track you are following skirts left of an isolated farm cottage to emerge on to a tree-bordered metalled road. Turn left to follow this over the old railway's tree-filled course. Now heading east under tall horse chestnuts, you soon emerge into the open and climb gently towards where sycamores and beeches cast their shadows across the tarmac. Directly beyond a lodge-type bungalow on your right the metalled road bends right and three unmetalled tracks diverge left. Take the middle one of these, which divides into two signposted rights-of-way within a matter of yards, at the foot

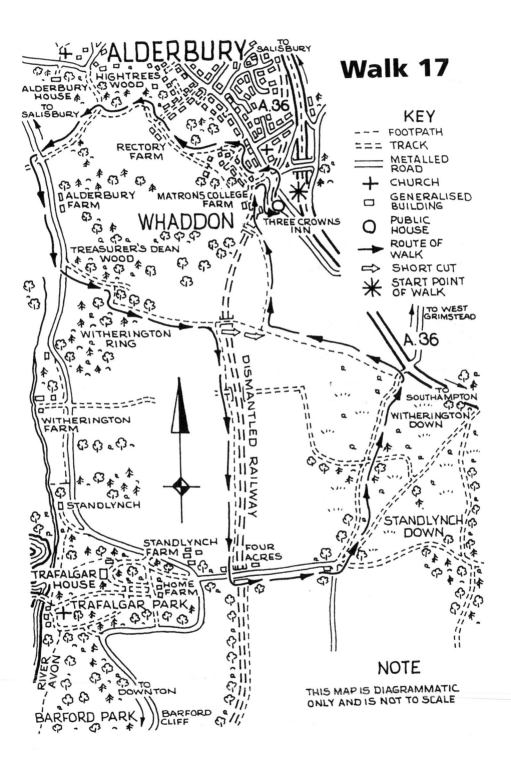

Walk 17

KEY

- – – FOOTPATH
- = = = TRACK
- ── METALLED ROAD
- ✝ CHURCH
- ▢ GENERALISED BUILDING
- Ⓠ PUBLIC HOUSE
- → ROUTE OF WALK
- ⇨ SHORT CUT
- ✳ START POINT OF WALK

NOTE

THIS MAP IS DIAGRAMMATIC
ONLY AND IS NOT TO SCALE

of Standlynch Down. Turn left here to follow a hard-surfaced track with trees on either side. Beyond a wooded dip where water collects in wet weather — it can be bypassed — you reach a track crossing and emerge into the open.

A fenced chalk track leads on ahead, climbing Witherington Down towards the A36 and its teaming traffic.

Looking east towards Pepperbox Hill

Within yards of this road turn left through a gate to follow a bridleway westward along the north margin of arable downland, with a low hedge and fence to your right. Here are the finest views on this walk, extending from Pepperbox Hill behind you across the undulating chalk downland and intervening Avon Valley to Clearbury Ring and its neighbouring high ground away to the west, ahead of you.

Carry on west along the field-edge to a gap through the hedge by a disused gate in its far right-hand corner. Pass through this to follow the left-hand edge of more farmland for a short distance before turning right to follow the unfenced grass track previously mentioned as the way back to Whaddon for those on the shorter route. After crossing a hump of arable downland this track descends and angles left, with a fence on your right.

The ivy-mantled brick parapets of a one-time railway arch precede a waymarking arrow pointing out the direction now to be followed, along a right-curving path over pastureland to the left of farm buildings. This brings you to a gate through which you pass to follow the right-hand edge of the next pasture to the next gate.

Here you emerge on to a farm road which you follow left-handed for a few yards to its junction with the road along which you first set out, by the sign pointing out the Pack Path — presumably one of those routes once used by packmen hawking their wares in remote country districts in the days when wheeled transport except on the roads between the bigger towns was a rarity. Turn right at the Pack Path's end to retrace your steps to the village road opposite Alderbury post office. Turn right here, then after a few yards fork right to follow the metalled path leading directly back to The Three Crowns and your car.

Chalkland Heights near Redlynch

WALK 18
Up to 4 hours
5 ½ miles
Walk begins page 111

Background to the Walk

Redlynch is the centrepiece of a complex of small villages east of the Avon, between Wiltshire's Downton and the Wiltshire-Hampshire border, which also marks the New Forest's northern boundary at this point. With names such as Morgan's Vale, North Charford, Hatchet Green, Hale, Bohemia and the ever intriguing Lover, these villages — some are mere hamlets — virtually adjoin each other while also contributing to the scattered nature of local development as a whole. Newhouse at Redlynch is a Jacobean house periodically opened to the public but there is not much else of historical note in the immediate vicinity. The parish Church of St Birinus, at Morgan's Vale, was built in 1894 at a time when local population was expanding fairly significantly and domestic building likewise.

While also partaking in many respects of the character of a typical Forest-edge village, Redlynch is almost as much a place of the Wiltshire chalk on whose edge it lies. This walk is essentially a chalk walk, with all this promises in terms of well-rounded hillscapes, valley views, hazy skylines and gentle agricultural countryside interspeded with burgeoning woodland abundantly populated with pheasants. Only one footpath stile is encountered, the route being largely one of those that make use of unmetalled lanes and bridleways in an area where human habitations are thin on the ground. Pleasant scenery and rural tranquillity can be looked forward to almost throughout, though peace is briefly interrupted when you cross and recross A36 near the

Maps
Landranger 1:50,000
Sheet 184
1:25,000 Explorer 130,
Salisbury and Stonehenge, and
131, Romsey, Andover & Test
Valley
Map Reference of Start/Finish
SU203213

How to get there
Redlynch lies on and adjacent to B3080 just over 1 mile east of Downton and nearly 2 miles from B3080's junction with A338, the Bournemouth-Ringwood-Salisbury road. From Southampton head west along A3024, M271 and M27 to Cadnam, then along B3079 to Brook, B3078 across the north of the New Forest to Bramshaw Telegraph and there fork right to follow B3080. Entering Wiltshire, this passes through Woodfalls to reach Redlynch, where you turn right to follow Grove Lane, a few hundred yards along which The King's Head lies back on your left. From Bournemouth follow Wessex Way and A338 to Ringwood, approaching which you briefly join A31 before resuming A338, which you follow north past Fordingbridge to its junction with B3080 on the western outskirts of Downton. Follow B3080 east and within 2 miles turn left at Redlynch to follow Grove Lane for a few hundred yards to The King's Head, on your left. Wilts & Dorset

services X7 from Southampton and X3 from Poole and Bournemouth connect at Salisbury and Downton respectively with services 43 and 44 to Woodfalls, which pass through Redlynch. Alight at Morgan's Vale crossroads and turn left to follow Grove Lane downhill to The King's Head, on your left as already mentioned. Walkers from Southampton can alternatively start this walk at Pepperbox Hill, a stopping-point for buses on Wilts & Dorset service X7 about halfway between Whiteparish and Alderbury.

Pub facilities
The King's Head

Run by Ann Halliwell who has made it enviably famous for good food, this 400-year-old hostelry has just about everything a country pub connoisseur could possibly wish for: suitable setting, unspoilt appearance, lengthy history as a pub and the welcoming atmosphere of a place where one can eat and drink enjoyably — but take car not to bang your head on those low beams! Weekday opening hours are 1100-1500 and 1730-2300, Sunday hours being 1200-1500 and 1800-2230. Food may normally be ordered at any time while the pub is open. The very comprehensive menu offers a choice of 11 starters ranging from avocado and crab or prawns, garlic bread and mushrooms and bacon in cream garlic sauce to prawn cocktail, prawns in filo dough with lemon mayo, smoked salmon and soup of the day. From 22 main meal dishes you may be tempted by barbecue ribs with fries, chicken breast with smoked cheese and ham sauce with veggies, sweet and sour chicken with rice, cod almighty with chips, gammon steak, egg and pineapple, mega

The King's Head, Redlynch

crown of Pepperbox Hill.

You do so on your way to and from The Pepperbox itself. From an altitude of 512 feet above sea level, this hexagonal brick tower, with its pyramidal roof, is a prominent landmark from miles around and a focal point of much curiosity by a ceaseless stream of visitors to the National Trust-owned downland upon the summit of which it looms. It is also known as Eyre's Folly from the probability of its having been erected by Giles Eyre, who died in 1655 and was 'a man much oppressed by public power' — or so says a tablet in his memory in Whiteparish church, two miles to the east.

Built in 1606, The Pepperbox (so-called from its shape) originally had six open arches spaced around its lower storey, with two windows, now blocked in, above each arch. Squire Eyre is supposed to have had it constructed out of envy of the towers of Longford Castle, in the nearby Avon Valley, but not perhaps solely as a 'folly' in the usual sense of a structure purely intended to round off a view and catch the eye. It is thought to have served a practical purpose, perhaps as a sheltered lookout point from which ladies could watch the progress of the hunt when hounds were operating near by. It looks to have been ideal in all respects for such a facility.

Without The Pepperbox as a focus of unending

fascination, perhaps the downland round about would not have survived in its present form as a pristine tract of unimproved grassland with associated flora, officially designated now as a Site of Special Scientific Interest (SSSI). The first steps to ensure this were taken in 1934 when a public appeal was launched and land was given by local magnates. In 1949 the 5th Earl Nelson rounded this off with a gift of The Pepperbox itself. Thus it was that Brickworth Down and West Dean Hill became a property of the National Trust and a place where botanists can still hope to find floral treasures like the harebell and the bee orchid as well as typical shrubs of the chalk such as juniper, spindle and wayfaring tree.

Walk 18

Distance: *Allow 4 hours for this five-and-a-half mile walk.*

Leaving The King's Head behind you on your left, head east along the adjoining road for a little way before turning left to follow unmetalled Sandy Lane. Houses flank this as it rises to a stile on your left, which you cross to follow the right-hand edge of a pasture, still heading uphill. A gate brings you out on to a lane which you follow right-handed past Templeman's Old Farmhouse, which lies to your right.

At this point the lane becomes gravelled and hedged with hazels as it heads into typical chalk country. A gently rolling pattern of large arable fields, thick hedgerows and patches of woodland spreads to the east, whilst to the west, as you gain altitude, the ground dips gently towards the Avon. The whole is suffused with a sense of remoteness. With not a human dwelling in sight once Templeman's Farm is well behind you, nor a single motor car within earshot, this is a countryside where anyone seeking a break from urban bustle can feel wholly at peace with the world.

Nearly a mile beyond the farmhouse you come a crossing of unmetalled tracks. Here you keep left-ahead to follow a rutted green lane which rises between tall hazel hedgerows. Gaps in the greenery to your left give increasingly scenic westerly views. Beyond the valley of the Avon, Clearbury Ring's topnotch of timber is a dominating landmark which reasserts its

mix grill with chips, pork steaks in Dijon mustard sauce, salmon and cream with prawns and veggies, sirloin steak with figs, mushrooms, tomatoes and onion rings or steak and kidney pie with veggies, to quote just a few. There are also five vegetarian dishes, three salads and eight different light meals ranging from ploughman's to home-cooked ham with two eggs and fries. There is also a choice of 11 sweets. A highly popular feature for which advance booking is strongly advised are theme nights on Monday when cuisine rotates between traditional Chinese, Italian and Indian food for which a small all-in charge is made, with customers helping themselves to as much as they like. All food prices are very reasonable and home cooking is the key to quality catering. Ushers' real ales are complemented by three draught lagers, John Smith's Bitter and Scrumpy Jack draught cider. There is a darts room but no jukebox, a pleasant garden for the warmer months and two log fires in winter, a family clientele being catered for. Walkers using the pub may leave their cars in the pub car park — but please ask first. The telephone number is 01725 510420.

The Pepperbox built in 1606

prominence every time you look that way.

Reaching a point where woodland flanks the right-hand side of the track, we paused to demolish picnic sandwiches while enjoying the undulating chalkscape. Pheasants spilled out from wayside hedgerows and a roe deer briefly foraged in the open while we watched. This is a spot where one could enjoyably soak up the scenery for hours.

Follow the green lane north through wood-edge beeches to where a gravel track emerges from the timber to your right. With gravel now underfoot, you keep straight on to a T-junction of gravel roads. Turn left here, then where the gravel road dips left within a few yards bear right to climb past a high ground reservoir. Once woodland passes behind, views open out as you head north along a fenced grass- and chalk-surfaced track. This converges with another track from your left as you approach a gate beyond which your track leads on through trees to reach A36 at the top of Pepperbox Hill.

Cross the wide and very busy road with great care to follow a hollow chalk track directly opposite. This leads to a car park close to The Pepperbox, having inspected which walk on a few yards farther, left-ahead, to where a direction indicator measures the miles to various places. In all but the murkiest of weather you should be able to see as far as Southampton Water in one direction and well beyond Salisbury in the other. To the south a dark smudge of dense timber announces the New Forest's northerly high ground, while another broad mass of woodlands clothes much of the lower land to the north, beyond which the chalk plateau of Salisbury Plain rears on the skyline.

If time and energy permit, take a leisurely stroll over Brickworth Down to seek out some of those floral delights which have helped to give it special status in the sphere of conservation. Then turn about to head back towards Redlynch, recrossing A36 where you did previously and then retracing your steps along

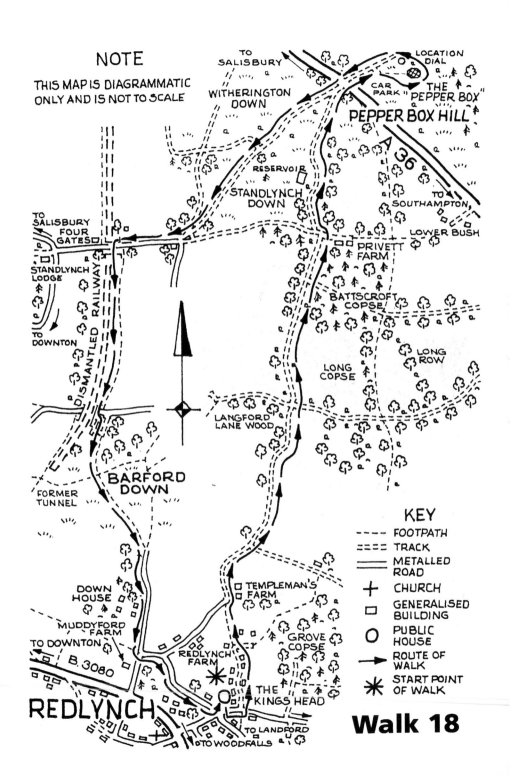

Walk 18

Witherington Down

the chalk track opposite. After passing through the gate a few yards along this, fork right from the track you followed on the outward stage of this walk to follow a grassy track which rises briefly before angling downhill and presenting dramatic views across the Avon Valley, to your right.

Towards the foot of a half-mile descent you pass through trees to reach a metalled lane at a point where it bends sharply. Passing an isolated lodge-type cottage on your left, follow the metalled lane right-handed, downhill, to the near side of where it bridges a tree-filled cutting where trains once ran. Here turn left by a bridleway signpost indicating the way to Redlynch to pass through a gate and follow a track along the right-hand edge of farmland. The bushed-in course of the old Salisbury-West Moors railway lies to your right as you head south, traversing three successive field margins before reaching another road with a tree-topped old railway arch to your right.

Angle left to cross the road and follow a grassy, hedged bridleway. Trees overhang this as it veers away from the former railway, diagonally climbing a ridge of chalk downland before following the right-hand edge of a field to converge with a chalk track which becomes a narrow, hedged lane as you follow it to the right. Take the first metalled lane that turns left from this, and where this soon forks bear right to follow a byway called The Row. This reaches Redlynch at a crossroads within yards of The King's Head, which lies directly to your left.

Ancient Forest Ways near Hamptworth

WALK 19
Up to 3 hours
4 ½, 5 or 6 miles
Walk begins page 116

Background to the Walk

Hamptworth's two syllables seem to duplicate each other's meaning and probably refer to an enclosed settlement once flanked by commonland on at least three sides: Hamptworth Common, Landford Common and North Common respectively. Hamptworth today is a scattered agricultural hamlet amid the heavily wooded countryside that extends several miles into south-east Wiltshire from the New Forest, with which it shares a number of features, including typical forest wildlife. Deer, for example, are no respecters of either forest or county boundaries and may be found in all these woods. We saw the fresh hoofmarks of fallow deer on farmland less than a quarter-of-a-mile from The Cuckoo Inn.

Landford dates back to Domesday, 20 years after the Norman Conquest, when it was recorded as 'Langeford'. By AD1242 it had dropped a 'g' to become 'Laneford', which seems to describe it to a nicety as signifying 'a ford crossed by a lane'. At that time Landford was within the Forest of Melchet which, with adjoining Clarendon Forest, formed a continuous royal hunting preserve linking up with the New Forest and extending almost to Salisbury.

The Landford of today consists in the main of modern dwellings in the midst of former commonland reclaimed for agriculture. This erstwhile open grazing ground is overlooked from a hilltop just beyond A36 by the parish Church of St Andrew, a bell-towered, stone-and-brick edifice in the Early English style which was rebuilt in 1858 on the site of a very much older church. Indeed, there has

Maps
Landranger 1:50,000
Sheet 184
1:25,000
Outdoor Leisure 22, New Forest, and Explorer 131, Romsey, Andover & Test Valley
Map Reference of Start/Finish
SU242198

How to get there
The Cuckoo Inn at Hamptworth lies on the Landford-Redlynch road, 1 mile west of Landford which is on B3079, the road that runs west and north from Cadnam by way of Brook and Bramshaw to join A36 a mile west of Plaitford. To reach Hamptworth from Southampton follow A3024, M271, westbound M27, and then A36, from which you turn left for Landford about 1 mile after passing The Shoe Inn at Plaitford and entering Wiltshire. At the next T-junction turn left, then take first right for Hamptworth where The Cuckoo Inn is on your right. From Bournemouth follow Wessex Way and A338 to Ringwood, there briefly joining A31 before resuming A338, from which you turn right at Downton to follow B3080. Within 2 miles turn left at Redlynch, beyond which you disregard a subsequent left turn for Whiteparish to reach The Cuckoo Inn almost 3 miles further on, on your left-hand side. Landford, an alternative

starting point, is served by alternate buses on Wilts & Dorset service X7 between Southampton and Salisbury, connecting at Salisbury with service X3 to and from Poole and Bournemouth.

Pub facilities
The Cuckoo Inn
This is an old style country pub 'in the middle of nowhere', and looks the part with its come-hither combination of thatch and brick and its four small rooms where customers congregate. This free house opens between 1130-1430 and 1800-2300 from Mondays to Fridays, all day Saturdays and Sundays and offers a choice of 8 real ales including Tanglefoot, Summer Lightning, Adnam's Broadside, Wadworth 6X, Pots Ale and GSB. Murphy's Irish stout, two lagers and Scrumpy cider are also on draught. Bar snacks are always available and include jacket potatoes, ploughman's and home-made pasties. Barbecues are a summer attraction. There is a garden and a play area for children. Dogs on leads are admitted and walkers using the pub may use the pub car park. The pub fields a cricket team and petanque is played here. Darts, dominoes and quiz nights all contribute to a lively social atmosphere enjoyed by both regulars and visitors. The building is well over 100 years old and at one time included a shop. The telephone number is 01794 390302.

probably been a church at this spot since before the Norman Conquest.

Landfordwood, to the north, is a scattered residential area two miles from the centre of Landford proper. It occupies part of the old Melchet Court estate, which was broken up in 1936. Melchet Court itself is now a special school. Melchet Park, in which it lies, is of very ancient origin. Once surrounded by the Royal Forest of Melchet, it was a medieval deer park in its own right. During the reign of Henry II his Chief Justice of the Forest, Alan de Neville, is recorded as having 'broken the park of Melchet', which 'caused the deer to go out', no doubt to the great annoyance of the local farming community whose crops the escapees would make free with.

Walk 19

Distance: *Allow at least 3 hours for the four-and-a-half, five or six-mile walks.*

There are two alternative starts to this walk, one being nearly half-a-mile longer than the other. The longer one begins by heading west towards Redlynch along the road from The Cuckloo Inn for about 200 yards to a gap in the hedge by a broken gate on your left. Go through this, heading more or less at right-angles to the road you have just left as you cross a field to pass through another gap towards the left-hand end of the hedge on its far side. You now enter a second field, the left-hand edge of which you follow, with a wood on your left. It was here that we saw fresh fallow deer hoofmarks: a salutary reminder that the New Forest and its fauna are only a couple of miles distant from this south-east Wiltshire farmland.

Directly beyond another hedge gap halfway along the length of the wood on your left you turn left at a crossing of paths to follow the new path into the wood. This path steers a well-defined course through encompassing timber before emerging between tall hedgerows on to a lane, which you follow left-handed. Within yards your lane joins another, which you follow to the left. Not many yards farther on turn right to follow a gravel lane, the shorter alternative approach to which is to turn left instead of right from The Cuckoo Inn and then immediately turn right to follow the road that leads to Nomansland. A little way along it this road bends right past farm buildings, then after a further very short distance you turn left by an electricity sub-station to follow the above-mentioned gravel lane, which is a public bridleway.

This unmetalled lane fords a brook at a watersplash which is bypassed on the left by a wooden footbridge. Having crossed this

The Cuckoo Inn, Hamptworth

you resume what is now a tree-shaded track of earth and gravel. Potholes which become puddles during wet weather can all be bypassed. Heading east, within a mile you emerge on to B3079 at Landford, an alternative place to start the walk for those who are using public transport. Here two more alternatives present themselves to walkers. The first is to follow the village road right-handed for a few hundred yards, past a wood on your left and some of the houses beyond, and there turn left to follow a gravel road signposted as a public footpath.

Beyond a metal gate where the gravelled way soon bends right, keep straight on along the left-hand edge of cultivated ground with a hedge to your left. This leads to a stile which you cross to follow the left-hand edge of a pasture to where the meadow-edge angles half-right. Here you cross on your left a rickety stile followed within a matter of yards by a further stile. From here we found the path's course lush with summer vegetation as we followed it straight on, to the right of greenhouses and other outbuildings of Park Farm, then along the right-hand edge of a paddock to a footbridge over a ditch followed by a stile leading out on to the Southampton-Salisbury main road not many yards east of a garden centre.

Turn right and then left to cross this extremely busy highway and follow a tree-hedged driveway which is also a public footpath. After passing the farmhouse on your right continue ahead through a gateway and carry straight on, with a hedge to your left. Beyond a further gateway your path angles slightly right before swinging left to cross the tree-bordered River Blackwater by a robust wooden footbridge.

You now follow the left-hand edge of a pasture uphill to a gate and a stile followed by a rising fenced track leading to Landford Manor Farm, with Landford Manor House on your left. After skirting the farm buildings you emerge on to a lane which you follow left-handed for a few yards to St. Andrew's Church and the view it commands across surrounding countryside.

We sat on a churchyard seat in the sunshine to enjoy our picnic lunch before backtracking to Landford village to check out the alternative route from there to the parish church.

Combined with the road approach from The Cuckoo Inn to the Hamptworth-Landford bridleway already described, this shortens the overall route to four-and-a-half miles. When you reach Lyndhurst Road (B3079) at Landford, cross it to follow a left-turning metalled footpath behind the houses flanking the road there, with fields on your right-hand side. This path re-emerges alongside the road, which you follow ahead for a short distance to a crescent of houses called Brookside. Leaving the road at this point, cross the green in front of the houses to pass a footpath sign on your left before joining a fenced path between a pasture on your right and a wooded gully along which flows the River Blackwater on your left.

This path is one where summer herbage grows profusely, so be prepared to cope with it if you walk here at that season, when a stick may well prove useful. The fenced path section ends at a stile where an arrowed waymark keeps you on course, parallel with the left-hand fence of the pasture you now enter as you head towards a farmyard. Here you follow some bordering railings to your right for a few yards to cross a metal-barred, wooden-stepped stile. A gravel track now leads you between the farmhouse and the outbuildings of Bridge Farm to another stile, beyond which you emerge on to A36. Follow the main road left-handed to cross the River Blackwater, then cross over when traffic permits and immediately turn right to follow a hollow lane uphill to Landford church and Landford Manor.

Here the alternative routes reunite as you carry on past the church and the manor house, or retrace your steps past these if you opted for the slightly longer approach already described. You then continue along the leftward-curving lane past Landford Manor farmhouse to where the lane soon bends sharply left. At this point you cross a stile on your right and head where the footpath sign here directs, across a pasture with a hedge at first on your left, and then straight ahead to another stile, on the meadow's far side. After crossing this turn right, with a bushed-in gully to your left and a fence to your right. This is another footpath section where summer herbage grows luxuriantly and may well need some subduing with a stick to ease your passage to where you fairly soon emerge among the outbuildings of Sandown Farm. Here you turn left through a gate to follow a rough-surfaced farm approach road.

This is flanked by scattered dwellings and acquires a metalled surface as it winds north-west between green fields with woods in the background and then past more scattered dwellings to where it is joined from the right by an unmetalled track and turns sharp left. The well-spaced houses of Landfordwood precede your emergence between stone pillars where once was a gated entrance to the grounds of Melchet Court. There was a corresponding entrance from Sherfield English, just inside Hampshire, the one you see here being in Wiltshire.

Beyond the twin pillars you rejoin the lane you left to follow the footpath to Sandown Farm. As you now follow it right-handed it skirts a small wood into which a signposted footpath turns right, offering yet another alternative route which you may wish to follow now, or possibly save for a separate outing to use in conjunction with earlier options already outlined.

For the five-and-a-half mile walk arrowed in black on the accompanying sketch-map, carry on downhill along Stock Lane, as the byway serving this outlying part of Landford proper is called. On being joined from the right by a metalled driveway after skirting the wood last mentioned, the lane bends left to reach A36. Cross this busy road with great care and climb a diagonally rising metalled path to reach a section of the old main road which was bypassed when A36 was widened and straightened here. Cross the old main road and head slightly right to join and follow left-handed North Common Lane, a gravelled byway, past the scattered dwellings of Northlands. Fields stretch to not-far-distant woods beside this lane as you follow it west.

After crossing a tree-bordered headstream of the River Blackwater you carry on through North Common Farm, where barking dogs may salute your passing. The public path leads through the farmyard, preceded and followed by metal gates. Beyond the second of these gates you follow a woodland track ahead to a crossing of tracks in a valley, where the slightly longer alternative route from Landfordwood and this one reunite. Those following the shorter route should turn left here, and then fork left where the track divides within a matter of yards.

If you opt for the longer walk, follow the signposted woodland path which turns right from Stock Lane just after leaving Landfordwood. A few yards along it the well-defined path divides and here you fork left. Soon you emerge from the wood on to a metalled lane which you follow right-handed for a few yards and then turn left to follow a grass-centred track with a garden on your right. This brings you to a gate alongside a stile with a waymarking arrow. Cross the stile, or pass through the gateway, and follow the arrow to head diagonally right across a meadow.

Go through or over a metal gate halfway along the length of the field fence now ahead of you, then continue across the next meadow to a stile with another waymarking arrow. This precedes a path fenced on the right and with scrub woodland and rhododendrons on the left of it. Your path soon joins a grass-centred track emerging from the left, and along this you continue ahead to where it becomes a gravel driveway serving various dwellings. Carry on along this to join and follow ahead a metalled remnant of the old A36 before its once twisty course hereabouts was straightened and widened. This emerges from flanking woodland to join the Earldoms-Whiteparish road, which you follow left-handed. A few yards short of where this joins A36 you follow a scrub-bordered track right-ahead — another fragment of the old main road — to reach and cross the busy highway a little way farther west.

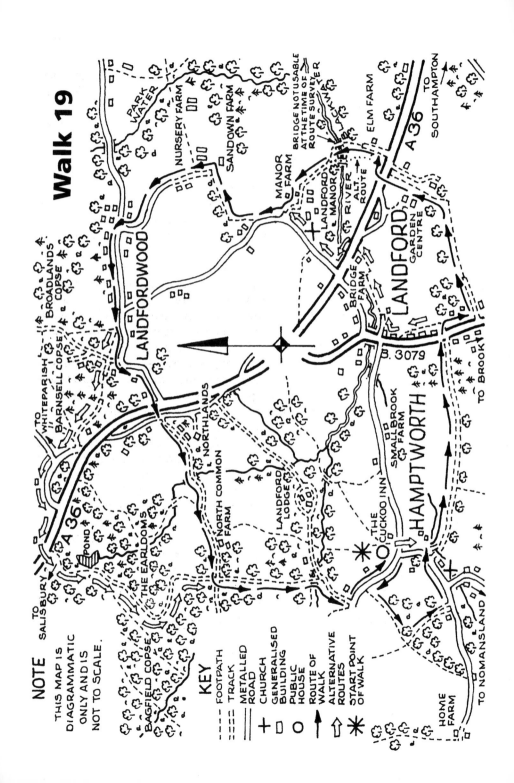

Follow the grass verge of A36 west for a few yards to a point directly opposite Glenside Farm, which lies to your right. Turn left here to follow an unsignposted track into dense woodland which the map reveals as extending for some three miles without a break: a sizeable chunk of the forest which once clothed much of south-east Wiltshire. Where the track soon forks, keep right. The track you now follow — a public footpath — curves left to skirt right-handed of the grounds of Earldoms Lodge. Just ahead now you ford a winding woodland brook — no problem in dry summer weather for those wearing shoes rather than boots — to carry on along a grass ride with well-grown timber trees to your left and the old oaks and hazel coppice of an area called Glazier's Copse to your right. The woodland to your left is called The Earldoms, recalling a time when an Earl of Pembroke had an interest in this neighbourhood.

Although no longer blessed with the title 'forest', this complex of coppice and plantations between the A36 and Redlynch remains a haunt of much forest wildlife. There have probably always been deer in these deep woods, and you will see signs of them in the form of well-worn ruts marking their crossing-points of ancient coppice banks, though perhaps not the elusive beasts themselves, at many points along this secluded section of the walk.

Where the ride forks keep straight on along a grass ride which continues ahead for half-a-mile or so and then circles left around a dark conifer grove to a crossing of tracks on the woodland's edge. Turn right to follow a tree-bordered track with meadowland on your left and woodland, at first, on your right, followed by one of the greens of Hamptworth Golf and Country Club.

The oak-and-hazel-hedged track leads you ahead to the valley track crossing reached by the shorter route not many yards past North Common Farm, and from which point directions for both are the same. A few yards ahead keep left where the track forks and carry on through woodland. Disregarding a subsequent right-turning track, you soon cross a stile and continue ahead. A pasture to your left precedes an area of replanted trees and then another stile. Your path is fenced from a pasture to your left as you descend to cross by a bridge one of the River Blackwater's headstreams. Here you join and follow right-handed a grass-centred lane which climbs between banks and hedges to emerge past golf club property on to the Redlynch-Landford road. Follow this left-handed past Hamptworth's Old Post Office Cottages with their thatch and herringbone brickwork, to arrive back at The Cuckoo Inn, where you started.

Wooded Ways around Minstead

Background to the Walk

Minstead is one of those communities which seem emphatically set apart from the outside world. Except for a tenuous link with Lyndhurst's surrounding fields and other enclosed land, it is completely encircled by forest and it is this, above all else, that makes it a little world apart, insulated from inappropriate, alien influences.

The *Victoria County History*, that unique window on Hampshire life as lived in the early years of the 20th century, refers to Minstead as a village of 'scattered deep roofed thatched cottages', and it is still such a place today. Modern building has intruded little. Picturesque ancient dwellings pop up around almost every corner: the enduring embodiment of an age-old way of life linked with the fields around and with the all-embracing Forest.

Minstead, in the main, has had a long, untroubled history since that one event which sealed it in public memory — the death by an arrow loosed accidentally or on purpose, supposedly at nearby Canterton Glen, of William Rufus while hunting one August day in AD1100. Whether this was the actual scene of the slaying is still disputed and will probably never be settled, although the iron plaque on Rufus's Stone hints at no doubts upon the matter.

Recorded in Domesday as 'Mintestede', meaning 'a place where mint is grown', there was probably a church here as well as a village in Saxon times. The present Church of All Saints, on its little, secluded hill not very far south of the village pub, owes something to various periods dating back at least to the 13th

Maps
Landranger 1:50,000
Sheet 195
1:25,000 Outdoor Leisure Map 22, New Forest
Map Reference of Start/Finish: SU282110

How to get there
From Southampton follow A3024, A35, Totton's southern and western bypasses and A336 via Netley Marsh before forking left for Bartley. At Bartley crossroads continue ahead into the New Forest, crossing A337 and then almost immediately forking left. At the next crossroads join a road which bends right as you follow it right-handed. The Trusty Servant pub is on your left by the next turning. If you turn left here you may find alternative parking space outside Minstead church, at the top of the hill. From Bournemouth follow Wessex Way east, A338 and then A31 to the beginning of M27 at Cadnam, where you turn off and take the third exit from the slip road. At the next roundabout take the third exit to follow A337 towards Lyndhurst, at the first crossroads along which you turn right. Directions thenceforward are as from Southampton after crossing A337. Solent Blue Line/Wilts & Dorset bus service 31A passes through Minstead en route from Southampton to

century and was originally thatched. It has several highly distinctive characteristics, not least its triangular arrangement of nave, chancel and a side chapel or secondary nave which almost exceeds the nave proper in dimensions. Georgian family pews for the local gentry, galleries once used by church musicians and to seat the parish poor including children from a local charity school, a 17th century three-decker pulpit, a font with a pre-Norman basin, a Norman chancel arch and a rare pre-Reformation church bell are other features, all adding up to a singularly delightful if decidedly unusual Hampshire village church interior.

The double lych-gate is modern, but the churchyard yew has been shown by a ring count to be around 400 years old. The ring count was made possible by some necessary surgery, the evidence of which is sadly all too plain to see.

Gravestones in the churchyard include at least one of a Purkess. It was a charcoal-burner named Purkess who is supposed to have carted the body of William Rufus to Winchester for burial, and the surname has remained common in the New Forest to this day. Also buried in the churchyard are various Comptons, a family whose heads were lords of Minstead manor for several centuries and who lived, as one would expect, in the Manor House. Another Minstead mansion, Castle Malwood, was built in 1892, taking its name from an ancient earthwork in the northern part of the area, the name Malwood being associated with that of Godric de Malf, who apparently held land here during the reign of Edward the Confessor. Castle Malwood is now the headquarters of Southern Electric.

Perhaps the best known Minstead resident of recent times was the man who created Sherlock Holmes, Sir Arthur Conan Doyle, whose home was at Bignell Wood, on the south side of the road between Brook and Cadnam. Sir Arthur died in 1930 at Windlesham in Surrey but was later reburied at Minstead along with his wife, who died ten years later. Their grave is under an oak tree at the far end of the churchyard.

The building in Minstead which perhaps excites more interest than most others is the pub, The Trusty

Lyndhurst. From Bournemouth, Wilts & Dorset service X2 calls at Cadnam, where connection can be made with Solent Blue Line/Wilts & Dorset service 31A for Minstead.

Pub facilities
The Trusty Servant
Minstead

This well-known hostelry, with its sign depicting a hog-headed retainer with explanatory verse opens on weekdays from 1100-1430 and from 1800-2300 and all day on Sundays from 1200-2300. Brews available on draught include Wadworth 6X, Gale's HSB, Ringwood Best Bitter, Fuller's London Pride, Guinness, Murphy's Irish stout and Stella and Heineken lagers. Thatcher's cider is also on draught here and there is a good selection of wines. There is an extensive restaurant area and a comprehensive a la carte menu offers a very wide choice of dishes ranging from home-made pies, scampi, cod and plaice to chillis and curries. Bar snacks include sandwiches, jacket potatoes, ploughman's and Yorkshire puddings. Chef's specials and vegetarian dishes are always featured. Children are admitted and there is a special children's menu. Food may be ordered between 1200-1400 and 1900-2200 (until 2130 on Sundays). Overnight accommodation comprises four double and three single rooms. Pub-using walkers may use the pub car park and there is additional parking space on the other side of the village green, on which summer fairs and morris dancing periodically take place. The telephone number is 01703 812137.

A Trusty Servant's portrait would you see,
This Emblematic Figure we'll survey.
The Porker's Snout not nice in diet shows,
The Padlock shut not secret he'll disclose.
Patient the Ass his master's wrath will bear,
Swiftness in errand the Stagg's feet declare;
Loaded his left hand apt to labour saith
The Vest his neatness, Open hand his faith.
Girt with his Sword his Shield upon his arm,
Himself and master he'll protect from harm.

Servant, with its sign depicting a bipedal pig-headed menial with ass's ears and the hoofs of a stag, attired in the Windsor livery of the time of George III. This is a copy of a portrait which hangs at the kitchen entrance in Winchester College, though it seems there is no special connection between the college and the pub except perhaps a shared sense of humour by individuals linked with each. The swine-snouted character with his pad-locked jaw, his wig, his sword and shield and his implements of work as a household servant is supposed to embody all the desirable qualities of a well-schooled retainer as envisaged by an artist of times long past who was also a wit as the appended verse shows.

Walk 20

Distance: *Allow 3 hours for this five mile walk.*

From The Trusty Servant follow the adjacent side lane uphill towards the church, passing Minstead's village green with its war memorial and well on your left. On your right are Crofton Cottages, built in 1897 as a technical school on a site given by the lord of the manor to mark Queen Victoria's Diamond Jubilee.

Spare time to visit the church with its cosy interior, to inspect the churchyard yew and to look for the gravestone of Conan Doyle and other more local notabilities before continuing through the kissing-gate to the right of the churchyard entrance. A fenced and hedged footpath leads you south-westward between pastures and through a brief section of Manor Wood, passing through a gateless gateway as well as a still-surviving gate before emerging through another kissing-gate on to a road in an area called Newtown.

Follow the road left-handed and cross a footbridge to the left of a watersplash ford, then bear left from the road to follow what becomes a parallel path. Where this path soon peters out as a visible footway follow the line of least resistance through old oaks and hollies between a woodland fence on your left and the rear of a dwelling facing the lane on your right. After a brief break the fence on your left reappears as you carry on over ground which after rain can be somewhat squelchy. Soon you enter a grassy clearing where you bear right to join a lane which branches left from the one you joined briefly by the watersplash at Newtown.

As you follow the lane on to which you now emerge left-handed it bends

The Trusty Servant, Minstead

right to pass a house called Muffins and a subsequent thatched dwelling, Woodbine Cottage, whose fairytale picturesqueness is marred only by an adjoining tiled extension. Yew Tree Cottage, not far beyond, is almost as visually appealing until you notice another tile extension, although this one is appended more discreetly to the rear.

Minstead Manor Wood lies to your left as you carry on to where your own lane joins another. Here bear right and head uphill to a crossing of lanes where you turn left. Now heading downhill, you pass Robins Bush Farm on your right before crossing a footbridge half-hidden behind bushes to the left of another watersplash ford. Your lane now rises past Acres Down Farm (bed and breakfast, cream teas!). Immediately beyond this, where a gravelly track turns left and another continues ahead into the Forest, follow a metalled road right-handed to a fork a few yards ahead, and there turn left to follow gravel road through hollies, tall oaks and beeches.

The gravelled way fairly soon veers right-handed to a gate where you enter Highland Water Inclosure, a wood as attractive as its name, thanks to the undulating variety of deciduous trees and conifers, ancient timber and young plantations, fresh and pleasing permutations of which confront you at every turn. Tall, dark pines, rugged Douglas firs and smooth-stemmed beeches, among others, alternate alongside the track you follow after disregarding a right-turning gravel track just inside the inclosure.

You now descend to cross Bagshot Bottom, along which flows Bagshot Gutter, a feeder stream of Highland Water. This latter turns out to be a youthful Lymington River, a name, however, which it disdains until enlarged by other tributaries, such as Black Water and Ober Water, north Brockenhurst.

Keeping to the gravel road via which you entered this woodland and which is signposted as a cycling route to Bolderwood, carry on to where another gravel road turns right, with a woodman's hut on its left-hand side not far along it. Turn right towards the hut, then almost immediately turn left along a green ride. Follow this ride, heading north-west in a straight line between lofty pines, climbing steadily at first, and then descending to join another gravel road.

Cross this to follow a gravel road which continues directly ahead in line with

Walk 20

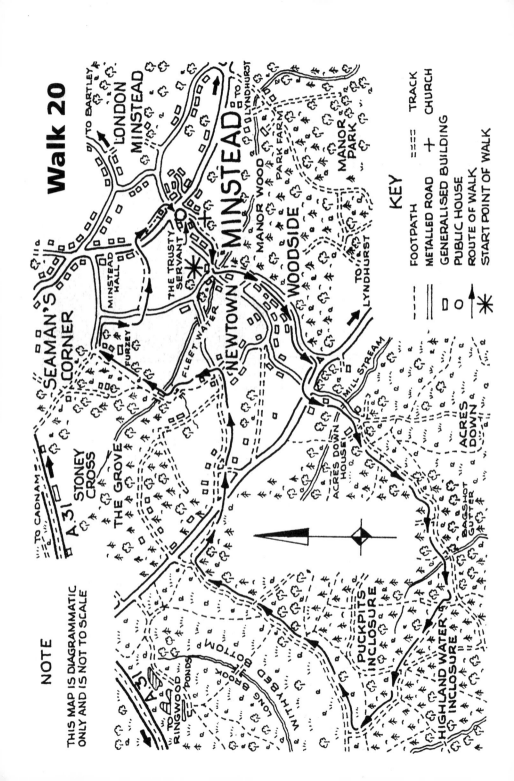

NOTE

THIS MAP IS DIAGRAMMATIC ONLY AND IS NOT TO SCALE

KEY

– – – – FOOTPATH	===== TRACK
METALLED ROAD	+ CHURCH
▯ GENERALISED BUILDING	
○ PUBLIC HOUSE	
► ROUTE OF WALK	
✳ START POINT OF WALK	

TO BARTLEY

LONDON MINSTEAD

MINSTEAD HALL

SEAMAN'S CORNER

TO CADNAM

A.31

STONEY CROSS

THE GROVE

TO CACNAM

FURZEY

FLEET WATER

THE TRUSTY SERVANT

MINSTEAD

TO LYNDHURST

MANOR WOOD

PARK FARM

MANOR PARK

WOODSIDE

NEWTOWN

TO LYNDHURST

MILL STREAM

ACRES DOWN HOUSE

ACRES DOWN

BAGSHOT GUTTER

LONG BROOK

WITHYBED BOTTOM

PONDS

RINGWOOD

A.31

PUCKPITS INCLOSURE

HIGHLAND WATER INCLOSURE

The Church of All Saints, Minstead

the ride you have just been following. Tall pines now spread to the right of you as well as to your left, where the ground slopes down into the valley through which flows the Highland Water, adding up to a scenically sylvan stretch equal to any on this walk. The gravel road ends at a turn-round point from which you carry on to a gate where you leave the inclosure.

The scene now changes dramatically, with tree-splashed Withybed Bottom forming the base of a heathland amphitheatre which cradles the Highland Water away to your left as you now turn right to follow a well-defined rising track, with the inclosure fence to your right. The far rim of the amphitheatre carries the A31 dual carriageway with its ceaselessly throbbing traffic, as marked a contrast as could be possible with the tranquillity close to hand.

Trees intermittently border your heathland track as you follow it up and over. Keep to the main track and avoid all minor ones until you emerge from some pines and hollies well within sight of a road ahead, where you bear right to follow a well-defined gravel path through a semi-open forest area of gorse bushes and scattered scrub. This path converges from the right with the Stoney Cross-Lyndhurst road, which you join and follow ahead to the end of a fenced wood on your left. Here you fork left to follow a signposted gravel bridleway, with fenced private property to your left.

By the entrance to a house called King's Garn on your left your track briefly

The grave of Sir Arthur Conan Doyle

ceases to be gravelled and winds through hollies before converging from the left with another gravel track, which you follow ahead. Bordering paddocks precede the point where the last few yards of your track are metalled and join a road.

Immediately upon reaching this road turn left to cross a stile and follow a signposted, fenced footpath between houses and their gardens. Fairly soon you bridge a stream and cross a stile to skirt the left-hand edge of a paddock with a fence on your right-hand side. This brings you to a further stile, after crossing which you turn right, as a yellow waymarking sign here indicates. Your path now descends through oaks and hollies to a stile and a handrailed plank bridge over a stream here called Fleet Water. This later matures as the Bartley Water to join the outflow of the Test between Eling and Totton, where it is spanned by an ancient toll-bridge near Eling tide mill.

Beyond this your path veers right and rises between more oaks and hollies, with a fence on your right-hand side. Soon you again turn right to pass through a walk-through stile and then carry on through yet more oaks and hollies to cross another stream by a plank bridge. After passing through another walk-through stile your path leads straight ahead to emerge by the entrance to Furzey Gardens, a centuries-old thatched cottage with grounds which are opened to the public.

Disregard a left-forking lane and follow the one that leads right-ahead here to converge with another from the left. Carry on for a short distance before forking right to follow a holly-bordered byway, not far along which you cross a stile by a footpath sign on your left to follow a path alongside the left-hand hedge of a sizeable pasture. A handrailed plank bridge and a further stile precede a paddock, the left-hand edge of which you follow to a stile preceding a lane. Follow this lane right-handed, taking advantage of a short parallel left-hand footpath before rejoining the metalled byway, which you follow ahead, descending past thatched cottages to a lane crossing where you turn right for The Trusty Servant and the end of this final walk in and around the delightful New Forest. I hope one and all will have given you pleasure and happy memories of one of England's choicest areas.